M000116678

The Comforter

Experiencing the Strength and Power of the Holy Spirit

Merton L. Clark

Interior & Cover Layout & Design:
Tarsha L. Campbell

Published by:

DOMINIONHOUSE
Publishing & Design, LLC
P.O. Box 681938 | Orlando, Florida 32868 | 407.703.4800
www.mydominionhouse.com

The Lord gave the Word: great was the company
of those who published it. (Psalms 68:11)

─────── ACKNOWLEDGMENTS ───────

I dedicate this book to everyone who desires to be filled and empowered by the Holy Spirit. Having an idea and turning it into a book is both internally challenging and rewarding. Thanks to everyone on the Communication & Promotion team at Truth Revealed International Ministries and DOMINIONHOUSE Publishing & Design, who helped make this happen.

"It was a moment pregnant with promise. Whatever Jesus was about to say to His disciples would change everything. The crescendo of events leading up to that moment would indicate there would be no turning back. Change was inevitable. The disciples felt it. They couldn't have been certain about how it would come, but they had their ideas about what would represent a cataclysmic shift, in their lives, community, nation, and possibly the world."

"Let us not overlook the momentous nature of the announcement. Jesus was introducing the Comforter. His ultimate aim would be to have them desire the gift of the Comforter and to anticipate the outpouring of this gift. But for the time being, His words were carefully crafted. He needed their faith to survive the events that would transpire in the days that would follow..."

Chapter 1

INTRODUCTION

He said unto them, Have ye received the Holy Ghost since ye believed? And they said unto him, We have not so much as heard whether there be any Holy Ghost. (Acts 19:2)

It was a moment pregnant with promise. Whatever Jesus was about to say to His disciples would change everything. The crescendo of events leading up to that moment would indicate there would be no turning back. Change was inevitable. The disciples felt it. They couldn't have been certain about how it would come, but they had their ideas about what would represent a cataclysmic shift in their lives, community, nation, and possibly the world. It probably centered around casting off the shackles of social and political oppression. Who could blame them? The world, as they knew it was one of injustice and struggle. As Jews living in the land of Israel under Roman imperial rule, they were second-class citizens in their own country. It was a night that would define destiny. History depicts that date as the night that Jesus was betrayed, unjustly tried, and crucified. From our vantage point in history, It's not hard to imagine the loud and dramatic events that led to Jesus' brutal execution. It has been depicted in many movies. By contrast, the hours before Jesus was violently taken into custody, was an evening of quiet conversation with His disciples. It could have been considered an evening that was no different from any other evening with the Master. Supper, instruction, reflection, and prayer was probably the normal order of any evening with Jesus. But there was nothing normal nor ordinary about the events that took place in the days and weeks leading up to that moment. Jesus had manifested great power and authority. He brought Lazarus back to life after being dead four days and then entered into Jerusalem triumphantly to a cheering crowd. Something big was about to happen. They waited intently for Jesus to unveil it. Despite being fraught with anticipation, the disciples did not know the extent or the magnitude of the change that would take place. They fully expected Jesus would unveil his plan to overthrow Rome, take the throne, and to set up His new government. In their minds, the time had come for all His talk of a coming Kingdom to come to fruition. It meant all the pillage, persecution, and pain of political struggle would be over.

To hear Jesus announce that evening, "Now is the Son of man glorified, and God is glorified in him" might have come as no surprise. What must have been alarming, however, was what He did next. Rather than prepare to clothe himself in the royal robes of a conquering king, He removed his garments, wrapped His waist with a linen cloth, and like a servant boy, stooped down, and washed their feet. Imagine their confusion. They anticipated He would ascend to Israel's throne, but instead, He went on that evening to speak as a departing friend. Imagine their disappointment. He warned of betrayal. Imagine their shock. He predicted His death. Imagine their despair. What could He possibly say next? He had promised a tremendous gift, and they sat and waited for Him to say what it would be. The last three years of His ministry, the last week of trial and triumph, the last few hours of confusion, despair and disappointed hopes all were a build-up to that present moment. Jesus unveiled His promise: the coming of the Comforter.

As we look back down the corridors of time some 2000 years and envision this story, it is easy to overlook the magnitude of what happened that night. Seated in our pews, hearing it read from the pulpit or discussed in a fiery sermon, we can easily dismiss the disciples as naïve. After all, they didn't have the 20/20 hindsight that time has granted us as spectators. It might be clear to us now that Jesus was referring to a paradigm shift and the disciples missed His point that night. We easily look back and think, Jesus came to establish a spiritual kingdom, not an earthly one. How silly of them to think his mission so mundane, so earthly and common. We grow so comfortable with the thought that the deliverance that Jesus came to bring has nothing to do with what we are experiencing here on earth. It is so easy to think, silly disciples. But were the disciples much different than we are today? Think of all the social injustices that surround us today. You often hear people rail against the establishment and lash out against the systemic nature of the injustices in this world. They believe the root of the injustices stems from the way oppression is ingrained in "the system." Is it far-fetched, as a follower of Jesus, to believe the deliverance He offers would extend to the very felt need for freedom on this side of eternity? Or was everything Jesus accomplished by dying on the cross to be enjoyed only when we all get to heaven?

I submit to you on that night in Jerusalem, Jesus was just beginning to set the stage for not only a shift in the paradigm of thinking on spiritual things, but to unveil the true magnitude of His victory. As He spoke to them, He figuratively painted pictures in their minds, and it was almost as if He made them feel a large creature that their eyes were too small to see. Carefully stopping to assure them, "you can't contain it now...but then you will. Don't be troubled...believe in me."

Let us not overlook the momentous nature of the announcement. Jesus was introducing the Comforter. His ultimate aim would be to have them desire the gift of the Comforter and to anticipate the outpouring of this gift. But for the time being, His words were carefully crafted. He needed their faith to survive the events that would transpire in the days that would follow so He prayed for them. Later as the conversation continued on the walk to the Garden of Gethsemane, He shared glimpses of the Comforter. He spoke of what the Comforter's role would be. They couldn't imagine anything better than having Jesus present in His physical body, walking alongside them, and performing miracles among them. But for the Comforter to come, Jesus would have to leave. How? When? They soon found out with a jolt of cold reality.

Suddenly, during the darkest hours of the night, Jesus was taken into custody, violently apprehended, and thrown before the authorities. The chief priests harangued Him, Pilate questioned Him, Herod mocked Him. The scene abruptly changed. Painfully, it went from the quiet of an evening stroll and prayer time in the garden, to a loud mob shouting, "Crucify Him, crucify Him, crucify Him!" The disciples were scattered, disoriented, and despondent. It seems that the quiet conversation about the Comforter was cast into oblivion in the face of the drama that was unfolding around them. Jesus was executed. The silence of disappointment and fear that came over His followers was deafening. It sent them into hiding. Any instructions He left them had scurried into a lockbox of doubt.

What could they hope for in the face of such deep disappointment? A "Comforter"? Would that be, perhaps, to comfort them as they endured the bitter pain of their shattered dreams of a coming messiah? Had the story ended there, the Comforter could be viewed as some sort of consolation prize. An impersonal, nebulous force meant to make them feel better that their hopes for a conquering messiah were dashed. Can you imagine such a scenario? Jesus would be viewed as a failure. He would be added to a long list of would-be messiahs of the day. Sure, they might claim to have freedom, but it would be reserved for some ethereal reality of "freedom" …perhaps in the world to come.

Can you imagine that? If it sounds tragic, it's because it would be. And yet, many believers unwittingly live their lives assigning a copacetic role to the Comforter or ignoring His existence altogether. But, praise God, the story didn't end there! Despite having been brutally assassinated, Jesus accomplished what had never been done before. He defeated death and rose triumphantly from the grave. What is the significance of the resurrection? How is this understanding related to receiving the promised Gift of the Comforter?

Jesus wasted no time in explaining to the disciples what had just transpired. On the day of His resurrection, He opened the scriptures and began to expound on the things concerning Himself. The conversation the night of his betrayal had only been an introduction to the Comforter. Jesus spent 40 days with His disciples after His resurrection. Have you ever wondered what Jesus and His disciples discussed for 40 days? What are the kinds of questions they might have asked Him? Scripture does not record all of their interaction with Jesus during these 40 days, but what we do know from the scriptural account, is that by the time Jesus left, no one intended to stop Him. The disciples had become so desirous of the promised Gift of the Comforter that they prayed non-stop. Have you ever desired a gift so intensely that you watched for its arrival intently? They gathered together in an upper room of a Jerusalem residence, watched and prayed for 10 straight days until the day the promised Gift arrived.

Jesus revealed to them the reality of the Comforter. They came to desire the outpouring and baptism of the Holy Spirit as a result of what Jesus was able to accomplish by His resurrection. The disciples did not have 2000 years of Christian culture and assumptions to draw from or, for that matter, be distracted by. Jesus would reveal to them the true identity of the Holy Spirit as He expounded on what the scriptures had to say about Him.

This book is designed to humbly take you into the experience of the followers of Jesus in the days after the resurrection. It will attempt to address out the scriptures questions that you might have as a believer today. Looking back at the story of the disciples in scriptures, there are many terms that we take for granted. They might be weighed down with so much implied meanings from generations of tradition and religious culture, that we seldom stop to ask what they truly mean.

The Christian life itself might be filled with assumptions of what to expect and what it should be. Many of these assumptions are founded on ideas that are not scriptural. Yet we don't stop to ask, is this how it is supposed to be, because we might unwittingly be relying solely on the experience of others. But what does the Bible say about the identity of the Comforter? Up until that point, the disciples had their Hebrew tradition, which referred to Him as the Ruach HaKodesh (translated, The Holy Spirit). Ruach HaKodesh was a general term used to refer to the spirit of inspiration from above, or the Divine Presence among the Jews, also known as the Shekhinah.

The hope is that as a result of reading this book, you will receive a scriptural understanding of the mission of Jesus, that inspire you to intently desire to be baptized and filled with the Holy Spirit and come to know Him intimately as the Comforter.

"The outpouring of the Holy Spirit was meant to restore all that Adam lost to Satan at the fall. To usher us into God's new reality, Jesus needed to first deal with the issue of the insufficiency of our composition. Dust is an inadequate container for the Spirit of God. The morning of His resurrection represented a new dawn for humanity."

Chapter 2

From "Dust" to Dawn

"For He knows our frame; He remembers that we are dust."

Psalm 103:14 NKJV

It is often said that the sky looks bigger in the Great Plains of the U.S. This effect may be a result of the land being flat. The flatness might force the eye to look farther to observe the horizon. One day out of the clear, big, blue sky, dark and terrifying clouds lined the horizon. As the massive clouds ominously rose in the distance, plain states' inhabitants braced themselves. Some raced home from their Sunday outings, thinking that a rainstorm might be approaching. Others did not know what to think. They had never seen clouds so black and so large and expansive. As the blackness neared, many wondered out loud if it was the end of the world. Sunday, April 14, 1935, was not the apocalypse, but it is recorded as the day America experienced one of its worst storms ever. It was no ordinary storm. It wasn't composed of the usual culprits that we associate with natural disasters. It consisted neither of rain, hail, nor snow. The agent of destruction was dust. It was a dust storm of epic proportions. The storm was so massive and intense that Timothy Egan, in his book, "The Worst Hard Time," notes the amount of dirt moved by the storm that afternoon doubled the amount that had been excavated to create the Panama Canal. The survivors' harrowing accounts tell of cattle dying, of autopsies done on horses that revealed their stomachs filled with fine dust, and of children slowly suffocating to death from what doctors came to refer to as dust pneumonia. What terror must have gripped the people of the high plains that afternoon as they were cloaked in darkness? They couldn't see their hands when they held them in front of their faces. Breathing, an essential act of life, had become life-threatening. Could they have imagined something so innocuous and normally so inoffensive as dust could potentially rise and choke the very life from their bodies? After all, dust only consists of particles of decayed fibers, such as fabrics and dead skin that we shed regularly. There is nothing more ubiquitous than dust. It's everywhere, but we hardly ever stop to consider what it is made of or how deadly it can potentially be. It goes unnoticed until it becomes a catastrophic event, as it did on that fateful day. "Black Sunday," as it came to be known, stands as a warning that even dust can be an agent of torment, danger, and death.

The storms of life can be very much like the dust storms that plagued the high plains in the 1930s. The seemingly dull challenges of life can converge to plummet life into a full-blown crisis. The stress of trying to cope can be suffocating and disorienting. For some believers, the storms of life arise so often that they find themselves relegated into survival mode. Church service becomes a fallout shelter as they move from one personal "Black Sunday" to another. Others struggle to gain control over the mundane elements of life. They can't seem to get their finances, relationships, or health under control. Yet, God did not intend for life to be a grovel in the dust. As Christians living in the fallen world, we will encounter trials and tribulations. Nevertheless, the Comforter's presence in our lives changes our position about the challenges of life.

Jesus accomplished a revolutionary change that would allow us to receive the Holy Spirit and allow Him to act as Comforter in our lives. It is a life where the Comforter uses the storms and challenges that will inevitably arise to draw the believer closer to God. He "flips the script" on suffering, if you will. It becomes an agent of spiritual growth to teach us and mature us in His ways and remind us of His promises. For a believer, life with the Holy Spirit is one of peace, destiny, and purpose.[1] Many believers, despite professing a belief in Christ, experience lives with high levels of confusion and wanton suffering. They seem easily subject to demonic oppression and defeat. They struggle with gaining victory over sin in their lives. They haven't tapped into the reality of the Comforter.

Just because a privilege has been made available to you, doesn't always mean you are fully enjoying it. Imagine you have been left an inheritance, but no one has sent you notice of it. While you struggle financially, maybe living from one paycheck to the next, a storehouse of funds might be out there with your name on it. If you are not aware of what is available to you, you do not know to claim it. Likewise, many believers are unaware of God's Gift and cannot reap the spiritual and natural benefits He provides. We must put aside the assumption that if we were born into church culture or have simply professed faith in Jesus sometime in life, there is nothing more to experience. In his missionary journeys through Asia minor, the Apostle Paul came across believers in a similar predicament:

He said unto them, Have ye received the Holy Ghost since ye believed? And they said unto him, We have not so much as heard whether there be any Holy Ghost.

And he said unto them, Unto what then were ye baptized? And they said, Unto John's baptism.

Then said Paul, John verily baptized with the baptism of repentance, saying unto the people, that they should believe on him which should come after him, that is, on Christ Jesus.

When they heard this, they were baptized in the name of the Lord Jesus.

And when Paul had laid his hands upon them, the Holy Ghost came on them; and they spake with tongues and prophesied.

Acts 19:2-6

These men were clearly believers, but they were ignorant of Jesus' revolutionary act. Subsequently, they could not take hold of what had been made available to them as a result. Although they were baptized for the remission of their sins, they lived as if the Holy Spirit didn't exist. Many believers are born into church culture. They might have heard the term "the holy spirit" tossed about. They may have even been baptized for the remission of their sins. If they are not aware of The Holy Spirit's true identity, however, they live not only as if The Holy Spirit doesn't exist but also as if the resurrection of Christ never took place. Their spiritual experience is truncated, and they become hindered by the storms of life.

There is no room for an attitude of general complacency in a walk with God. He intends for the experience of the believer to be a progression from one level of glory to the next.[2] God always has more for His children to experience in their spiritual lives. The true gems are reserved for those who ask. There are things in life that a believer will only experience if the attitude of complacency is completely set aside. The Comforter is a gift that is reserved for those who ask. Many don't know to ask for the Holy Spirit. We cannot underestimate the importance of asking.

"If you then, though you are evil, know how to give good gifts to your children, how much more will your Father in heaven give the Holy Spirit to those who ask him!"

Luke 11:13 NIV

The disciples spent time learning from Jesus about the Holy Spirit before the desire for the Gift burned in their hearts. Their desire led them to pray earnestly for His arrival. Prayer is petitioning God for His divine intervention. There is no doubt that as a loving Father, God wished to lavish this Gift upon them. Why would it be important for them to ask?

Some people are sitting back, waiting for the Holy Spirit to act on their behalf without beckoning. They take His presence as a "given" of simply professing belief in Jesus. But there is a process of asking that the Father requires; a level of desire that must be inherent in you for Him to step in and offer His assistance. It reminds me of a day when my young son joined me outside as I raked leaves. He was only a small child at the time, but he was eager to be a part of what was going on. As I began raking and filling bags to place them on the side of the road, I watched my son struggle to grab one of the bags. He lifted it off the ground, then put it down again. He picked it up again and again. With each lift, I watched his strength diminish. He seemed so happy to have me watch him work, probably thinking of how proud I was to see him do it on his own. Soon it became pretty evident he needed help, and yet, as a father, I could only allow myself to step in if, and only if, he would ask. I was there the entire time, but he refused to ask for help. Instead, he struggled until his, strength was completely spent.

When lifting the bag did not work, he decided to drag the bag across the lawn. This second strategy went on for some time, but it left a trail of leaves behind. It was not until he began tumbling over the bag a few times that he surrendered to the idea that he needed help. He said, "Dad, help me." I smiled and replied, "I was wondering when you were going to ask for help." My response confused him, and he asked, "If you knew I needed help, why didn't you just help me?" I answered, "Because you didn't ask."

Similarly, God's Fatherly love causes Him to wait for us to seek Him for help. He is gentle and will not impose Himself on us. For the sake of our growth and maturity, He wishes that we will ask. Maybe because our growth is contingent upon our first learning the limits of our own strength. Nevertheless, He promised that He would answer when we call.

"Then you will call on me and come and pray to me, and I will listen to you. You will seek me and find me when you seek me with all your heart."

Jeremiah 29:12-13 NIV

There is a level of experience that is available to the believer only when earnestly sought out. It is our responsibility to take hold of His promises. We must desire, we must seek. We must ask.

Although difficult to endure, dust storms can wake our consciousness to our need for God. Amid storms, we begin to ask ourselves questions about our existence. We seek and desire a change in our circumstances. Storms can prompt us to seek more of God. The Bible tells the story of Jabez. The Hebrew meaning of his name is pain, trouble, or sorrow. Imagine being named after utter grief? Jabez noticed the trend of events in his life reflected the awful meaning of his name.

It is not clear whether Jabez had a consistent prayer life or whether this was his first prayer. Nevertheless, it was recorded that he asked God for divine intervention in his life:

"And Jabez called on the God of Israel saying, "Oh, that You would bless me indeed, and enlarge my territory, that Your hand would be with me, and that You would keep me from evil, that I may not cause pain!" So God granted him what he requested."

1 Chronicles 4:10 NKJV

It was a prayer that turned his destiny around and snatched it from the hands of dishonor and defeat. In the end, the Lord granted his request. God enlarged the boundaries of his influence and the Lord stayed with him. His prayers made him more honorable than his brethren. The pain and the storms in Jabez's life caused him to dare to ask God, and God intervened.

Do not underestimate the need and the power of asking. The Comforter is the Gift that is meant to guide us into a life of victory above all of life's circumstances. It is only by receiving and coming to know Him that we can live a life of reaping the rich benefits of Jesus' finished work. It is a life of peace above the dust storms of life, not a futile existence of staggering helplessly amidst them.

The disciples had been sorrowful and distraught at the crucifixion of Jesus. They were in the midst of their dust storm of fear, doubt, and uncertainty. In His Fatherly love, God allows the storms of life. But He promises:

"Weeping may endure for a night, but joy comes in the morning."

Psalm 30:5 NKJV

The morning of the resurrection, their grief was turned to joy. When the day of Pentecost came, the followers of Jesus were gathered in the upper room of a Jerusalem residence. They were intently engaged in the act of asking.[3] Their desire was no doubt nurtured by the knowledge and instruction they received from the resurrected Christ.[4] They prayed expectantly. In so doing, their hearts were fertile soil for the birth of the church. The Holy Spirit was poured out on all the earth that fateful day. Those in the upper room were the ones who were in the posture to receive Him. Their lives were never again the same because they had learned to desire, ask and seek after the Gift of God. As a result, they ushered in an era of a new dawn for all humanity.

The resurrection was a sweeping, revolutionary accomplishment. Jesus had secured all the benefits of a new life in the Spirit for all humanity. But it will only be manifest in the lives of those who learn to desire, seek, and ask for more in an experience with God.

We can credit the dust storms of life for creating the needs that compel us to yearn for more from God. In the middle of storms, we might think, "there has got to be more to life than this," and intensify our pursuit of God as a result. Another thing the storms of life will do is make us question what we are made of. When caught in the thick of things, we tend to come in contact with our very human vulnerability.

The act of pondering our existence can be a hopeless and depressing exercise. Without divine revelation, there is no true insight into the question of the human condition. There is no way to understand the dreadfulness of our plight from heaven's perspective. Our nature becomes the standard for what we might begin to consider divine.

Think of the false stories from mythology that survive till the present day. They tell of gods whose natures reflect tendencies common to fallen human nature: Lust, greed, envy, jealousies, etc. They are not gods at all but the figment of human imagination![5]

It is no wonder that throughout human history, many theories have arisen as to our origins that just seem bizarre in the modern-day. We need revelation from God even to begin to consider our composition.

In His now famous conversation with Nicodemus, Jesus explains the spiritual inadequacy of our fallen human composition. Nicodemus had sought Jesus under the cloak of night. He probably chose to approach Jesus in the dark, hoping to avoid compromising his high status as a Pharisee (a religious ruler) among his people. Jesus must have been viewed as a controversial figure among the religious erudite. No doubt for His claiming to be the Son of God, while lacking a formal degree of religious training, by their standards. Still, no one could deny that God was with Jesus because His ministry was followed with signs and wonders. Nicodemus probably expected to glean some spiritual insight from Jesus in a short conversation. Perhaps Jesus had tapped into a habit or an approach to God yet unknown to him in all his learning, he must have thought. Imagine his surprise at being confronted by Jesus about the insufficiency of his very nature. In His conversation with Nicodemus, Jesus wasted no time in emphasizing that human inadequacy goes far beyond the struggle to stay above the dust storms in life. His human composition denied Nicodemus the connection with God that he so desired; the relationship that he observed Jesus had with the Father. Jesus was telling him that despite his best effort at religious excellence, at his core, he could never be good enough of a vessel to contain the Spirit of God. Imagine how difficult it must have been for Nicodemus to understand what Jesus was saying? Jesus was unveiling the need for a completely new version of man, one made of spiritual substance. It's not like it would be a transformation that could result from a change in attitude or by developing a new habit or ritual. He was saying that our very composition is inadequate to experience God. Nicodemus must have thought, how on earth would we go about effecting a change in our very composition. It's not like we can go back in the womb of our mothers again. But the transformation needed would be so radical that rather than a "do-over," the new birth would be an entirely new experience.

"That which is born of flesh is flesh, that which is born of the Spirit is spirit."

John 3:6

There was nothing Nicodemus could do that night to experience this new birth. In fact, there is nothing inherent in any human being that would make him able to accomplish this feat. Jesus first had to make it available by His death and resurrection. It would only be by putting faith in the finished work of Christ that the experience of the new birth would be made possible.[6] Jesus would have to usher in a new version of mankind, one capable of accommodating the indwelling Spirit of God. Jesus was giving Nicodemus insight into the ultimate purpose of His mission. Through His suffering, death and resurrection, a way would be made for humanity to be restored to a relationship with God, one that mirrors the intimate relationship that He experiences with the Father.

"But as many as received him, to them gave he power to become the sons of God, even to them that believe on his name:

Which were born, not of blood, nor of the will of the flesh, nor of the will of man, but of God."

John 1:12-13

Life in the Spirit is one of living out the destiny God has purposed for you. Life without the Holy Spirit is a life of merely coping; being too preoccupied with storms, and common challenges of life to even think of purpose.

The psalmist decries our very composition as human beings:

"For He knows our frame; He remembers that we are dust."

Psalm 103:14 NKJV

Imagine the ramifications of being "dust." If the dust storms of our lives arise due to our fallen human nature, how can we ever hope to have any command over them? Dust has no rank over dust. The outpouring of the Holy Spirit was meant to restore all that Adam lost to Satan at the fall. To usher us into God's new reality, Jesus needed to first deal with the issue of the insufficiency of our composition. Dust is an inadequate container for the Spirit of God. The morning of His resurrection represented a new dawn for humanity. It meant not just a guarantee of eternal life in the spirit realm, but also a victorious spirit-led life in the present for each believer. By making it possible for human beings to receive and contain the Holy Spirit, Jesus brings not only a conquest over death in the future, but an upgrade to the human experience in the present life.

Notes

1. Romans 8:6-10

2. 2 Corinthians 3:18

3. Acts 1:14

4. Luke 24:27

5. Isaiah 40:18-22

6. John 3:14-17

Dust storms in life create the need to yearn for the Comforter.

***

"For He knows our frame; He remembers that we are dust."

Psalm 103:14 NKJV

"As the new wine continues to bubble, the wineskin would expand. If the wineskin were old, it would have already been expanded to its maximum capacity. It would then not be able to stretch to accommodate the fermentation process. It would therefore burst, and the wine would be wasted. New wine, therefore, needed new wineskins..."

Chapter 3

NEW WINESKINS

"And no one puts new wine into old wineskins: otherwise, the wine will burst the skins, and the wine is lost, and so are the skins: but one puts new wine into fresh wineskins."

Mark 2:22 NIV

When a new version of technology is released, it is usually accompanied by a lot of hype. The manufacturer launches a marketing campaign to make the release date of the new device feel like an event. Every means is employed to showcase and promote their latest phone, application, or gadgetry. You can hardly drive anywhere without seeing the "coming soon" style announcements on billboards. Neither can you turn on the television without coming across the commercials about it. Despite all the manufactured hype, none show more enthusiasm about the new version's release as the owners of the current and previous versions. They are intimately acquainted with all the older version features, but more importantly, they are aware of its limitations and shortcomings. They can truly anticipate the improvements the new version will bring. Jesus is referred to as the second Adam. Similarly, we can't truly appreciate the need for a second Adam until we understand the experience and shortcomings of the first.

29

Adam, was the first man to be created and the father of us all. He ate the forbidden fruit and was banished from the garden of Eden as a result. His rebellion also meant death would ultimately become the plight of all humanity. It's not difficult to look around and recognize the physical results of this fall from grace. Death and large-scale destruction are the subjects of most news reports these days. Also, the common challenges of life like illness, job loss, death of loved ones, divorce, disappointments, etc., affect us all in one way or another. We can all blame Adam's disobedience for the trouble. But what were the spiritual ramifications of Adam's sin? Adam was warned that the day he should eat the fruit, he would die. Scripture records, however, after he rebelled, though he was banished from the garden, Adam went on to have children and die at the age of 930. So, did he die on that particular day that he sinned, as God warned him? It might surprise you to know, that he, in fact, did. That very day, his spirit died. His true God-ordained essence was lost and so was his ability to be under God's governance. To God, spiritual life is life. When Adam ate the fruit, he stopped blinking on heaven's radar. The whole world came under a thick cloak of darkness.

"Adam, where are you?" God called out as He walked in the garden in the cool of the day. Why would the all-knowing God appear not to know where Adam was? Adam had now become a shell and a shadow of his true existence. He was only identifiable by his physical nature–dust.

"From dust you came, to dust you shall return."

Genesis 3:19

It is as if God was describing Adam's unraveling. The human experience was relegated to being marked by dust. Mankind would have to toil to bring about mere sustenance. Despite the nuisance dust would become to Adam, it wasn't God's intention that he be dominated by it. The curse of floundering in the dust was given to the serpent.

"...Because thou hast done this, thou art cursed above all cattle, and above every beast of the field; upon thy belly shalt thou go, and dust shalt thou eat all the days of thy life."

Genesis 3:14

The dust is for bottom dwellers, not high risers. God's intention was for Adam to live above the mundane challenges of life. Before the fall, Adam had been given authority to speak and dictate his circumstances and surroundings. He organized and oversaw the destiny of every created thing. Though formed in the dust, he was not at his essence, dust. His makeup was made more complex to reflect the very image of God.

Some people are comfortable considering humans as just an intelligent form of an animal, no different from the beasts of the field. They point to the similarity in biological functions humans share with other creatures. Nothing could be further from the truth. Before we settle for being deemed simply "dust," Let us examine God's original intention by revisiting the creation story more closely:

Picture God was stooping down and physically molding the first man, Adam, from the dust of the ground. He then breathed into the nostrils of man and made him a living being. No other creature came about as a result of a direct touch from God. No other creature shared God's very own breath. Let's explore that distinction. Breathing. All living creatures "breathe" in some form or other. Even plants "inhale" carbon dioxide and "exhale" the oxygen we all need to survive in the natural realm. Their ability to breathe came about as a result of God simply speaking them into existence. Adam, on the contrary, came about by a more intimate process. He was given a spirit that came directly from God, which made him, in essence, a spirit-being that resided in a body and had a soul. What distinguished mankind from other creatures is the mechanics employed by the Creator in making him and the rights and privileges that He afforded to him. Mankind was made in the image of God. He was made creative, productive and in charge of his environment.[1]

By design, man had been given the true breath of life–spiritual life. God is Father, Son, and Holy Spirit. Man was made comprised of spirit, soul, and body.

What would it mean to have dominion over nature? What is it like to be about the business of dictating destiny to your surroundings? We can imagine this reality in a metaphorical sense. We see the storms of life subsiding at our command. Wouldn't that be great? In the gospel accounts, however, we see Jesus demonstrating a direct supernatural command over nature. When He said, "peace be still," the literal waves and winds obeyed. Fishes and loaves multiplied in His hands and at His command, blindness and leprosy would flee. His works were utterly phenomenal. It inspired men to ask, "what manner of man is this?" He was a new version of man…the second Adam.

Was Jesus a sort of superhero, as we see depicted in very popular films of the day? Did He innately possess qualities that allowed Him to perform superhuman feats? Did the Holy Spirit serve as an impersonal force that just "empowered" Him to do miracles? These questions are addressed in the gospels because frankly, the people of the day were astonished at the signs and wonders that followed Jesus in His ministry and so they challenged Him about it. When Jesus was questioned about the source of His authority, He credited His Father and the Holy Spirit for the acts of His ministry. His power came directly from a continuous, loving and deeply relational connection with the Father made possible by the Holy Spirit.

"So Jesus replied, Truly, truly, I tell you, the Son can do nothing by Himself, unless He sees the Father doing it. For whatever the Father does, the Son also does. The Father loves the Son and shows Him all He does. And to your amazement, He will show Him even greater works than these..."

The Holy Spirit allowed Jesus to maintain and nurture intimacy with His Father. In fact, Jesus maintained the habit of retreating into nature to pray and spend time with the Father.[2] It was His intimate and abiding connection with the Father that was the source of all the power.

The disciples must have felt invincible with Jesus by their side. It's not difficult to understand their disappointment at the last supper when Jesus made clear His impending departure. In their minds, Jesus possessed the power to change their circumstances, and now He would leave. Jesus wished to impress upon them the idea that His departure would make provision for the power to also rest on them.

"Very truly I tell you, whoever believes in me will do the works I have been doing, and they will do even greater things than these, because I am going to the Father."

John 14:12, NIV

He was leaving them, to suffer and die on the cross. At this point in their journey, they believed that Jesus was the Son of God. Jesus was divine and shared an intimate bond with the Father. They were unaware, however, that the scriptures foretold that Jesus must first suffer, die and resurrect to complete His mission.[3] Though they had put their faith in Him, they had very little understanding of his true mission.

Jesus, being God, was also fully human. The Holy Spirit conceived him in the womb of a virgin.[4] He was sinless and came from an incorruptible seed. His divine identity as the only begotten Son of God and his humanity would set the stage for the resurrection to create a cataclysmic shift in the spirit realm. The disciples had no idea their faith would soon serve as a birth canal into a new reality.

Jesus took the penalty for sin for all humanity. By His resurrection, He opened an avenue into a new life for humanity. As the merit of His death and resurrection, He extended all the rights, privileges and abilities of His Sonship (being a child of God) to all who would believe in Him. This would include the ability to possess the indwelling Spirit of God, perform great exploits, and the ability to rise from the dead.

"But now is Christ risen from the dead, and become the firstfruits of them that slept. For since by man came death, by man came also the resurrection of the dead. For as in Adam all die, even so in Christ shall all be made alive."

1 Corinthians 15:20-22

When believers pray in the name of Jesus, they take on His divine identity before the eyes of the heavenly Father. They are essentially asking God to consider the request as if Jesus Himself is submitting it. They are asking for Him to take into account the most intimate bond that exists in the universe. Jesus is the first of a new version of humans, possessing the capability to be intimately connected with the Father.

Everything Jesus did on earth was meant as an example to His followers. It was meant to demonstrate to them what capabilities would be available to them as children of God. His disciples needed the Holy Spirit to provide the atmosphere in which to engage with the Father. But first, Jesus needed to make it possible for each believer to become a suitable vessel to contain the Holy Spirit.

Throughout the scriptures, the Holy Spirit is metaphorically or symbolically referred to as liquid. Jesus referred to Him as rivers of living water.[5] He is also referred to symbolically as oil. When God describes His intention of giving the Holy Spirit to His people, He uses the verb "pour." The following are some examples:

"For I will pour out water on the thirsty land And streams on the dry ground; I will pour out My Spirit on your offspring And My blessing on your descendants;"

Isaiah 44:3 NIV

"And it shall come to pass afterward, that I will pour out my spirit upon all flesh; and your sons and your daughters shall prophesy, your old men shall dream dreams, your young men shall see visions: And also upon the servants and upon the handmaids in those days will I pour out my spirit."

Joel 2:28-29

And I will pour upon the house of David, and upon the inhabitants of Jerusalem, the spirit of grace and of supplications: and they shall look upon me whom they have pierced, and they shall mourn for him, as one mourneth for his only son, and shall be in bitterness for him, as one that is in bitterness for his firstborn.

Zechariah 12:10

Liquid is probably the best form suited to capture the behavior and qualities of the Holy Spirit. It is also suitable to describe the experiences the believers have as a result of the Holy Spirit acting in or upon them.

Jesus used an illustration from agrarian life to describe the disposition necessary to be open to receiving the Holy Spirit. In the following illustration, wine represents the Holy Spirit, and wineskins represent the mindset of a would-be believer:

"And no one puts new wine into old wineskins: otherwise, the wine will burst the skins, and the wine is lost, and so are the skins: but one puts new wine into fresh wineskins."

Mark 2:22 NIV

In this verse, Jesus explains that new ideas cannot be put into old ideologies. For this reason, old ways of thinking must be abandoned to receive new ways of thinking.

Nowadays, it is difficult to imagine what life was like before refrigeration. The modern amenities of life can easily make us far removed from the illustrations we see in scripture that derived from an ancient society. Wineskins were bags traditionally made of leather to hold wine. Bota bags, the traditional Spanish liquid receptacle, survive today as an example. Whenever new wine was made, it was fresh and would not yet be fermented and preserved. The magic would be observed in the way the wine ferments within the wineskin. During fermentation, the natural sugars in the wine turn into ethanol and carbon dioxide and begin to bubble. As the new wine continues to bubble, the wineskin would expand. If the wineskin were old, it would have already been expanded to its maximum capacity. It would then not be able to stretch to accommodate the fermentation process. It would therefore burst, and the wine would be wasted. New wine, therefore, needed new wineskins as a receptacle if it would ever serve its intended purpose. The people to whom Jesus was addressing this illustration were religious rulers. They could not recognize Jesus as the divine Son of God because of their religious paradigm of thinking.

"You search the Scriptures because you think that in them you have eternal life; it is these that testify about Me; and you are unwilling to come to Me so that you may have life."

John 5:39-40 NASB

Their inflexibility was due to approaching God from the vantage point of their understanding. Dust is an inadequate vessel to contain the Spirit of God. Their dusty approach to God centered on focusing on the past. They were resistant to anything new. Their inability to accept God in a new way would alienate them from receiving spiritual things. New wineskins represent the new birth experience. Wine represents the indwelling presence of the Holy Spirit and His growth-oriented work in the believer. Many times, what keeps people from receiving the Holy Spirit is their grip on religious tradition. They don't want to let go of their old view of God that has been passed down from generation to generation and embrace a new thing. God says:

"Remember ye not the former things, neither consider the things of old.

Behold, I will do a new thing; now it shall spring forth; shall ye not know it? I will even make a way in the wilderness, and rivers in the desert."

Isaiah 43:18-19

The religious rulers were unwilling to come to Jesus and accept Him as the savior because it meant giving up the old way of thinking about religion. Their old way of thinking about God centered on obsessing over minute details in keeping Moses's law. But God had long since announced to their fathers through the prophet Jeremiah, that there would be a revolutionary change:

"Behold, the days are coming, declares the Lord, when I will make a new covenant with the house of Israel and the house of Judah, not like the covenant that I made with their fathers on the day when I took them by the hand to bring them out of the land of Egypt, my covenant that they broke, though I was their husband, declares the Lord. For this is the covenant that I will make with the house of Israel after those days, declares the Lord: I will put my law within them, and I will write it on their hearts. And I will be their God, and they shall be my people. And no longer shall each one teach his neighbor and each his brother, saying, 'Know the Lord,' for they shall all know me, from the least of them to the greatest, declares the Lord. For I will forgive their iniquity, and I will remember their sin no more."

Jeremiah 31:31-34 ESV

NEW WINESKINS | 39

They were so myopic in their thinking they overlooked the prophecies about Jesus. The new thing that God would do would be centered on an internal and dynamic experience with Him. They refused to accept Jesus because they clung to the external trappings of religion. They weren't willing to consider that their ideas about the coming Messiah were wrong.

Believers today might have picked up ideas about Jesus from their religious tradition. Some of these views are unscriptural. They might deny or overlook His divinity as the Son of God or diminish His role in the life of a believer. To access the experience that God has in store, you must be willing to challenge your old ideas about Jesus. Examine His claims. Meditate on His mission and His work. You must be willing to abandon old ideas and allow yourself to see Him with new eyes.

"But we all, with open face beholding as in a glass the glory of the Lord, are changed into the same image from glory to glory, even as by the Spirit of the Lord."

2 Corinthians 3:18

The journey of the believer is meant to be a progression of increasing glory. Peer into the person of Jesus. The religious people of the day were combing scripture for new ideas to reinforce their old ideologies. They were not looking for God. Had they been searching for a personal encounter with God, they would not have missed Jesus. Are you personally searching for God, or are you comfortable with ideas you have about God? Do not let old ideologies keep you from experiencing a new thing with God. Ask God for a burning desire to know Him personally. He will reveal Jesus to you.

It is only by putting faith in the finished work of the Lord Jesus that we can receive the Holy Spirit and begin to truly understand the things of God. Jesus is the door into an experience with God.[6] The experience of the Holy Spirit is often out of reach to people because they attempt to understand God without first receiving the new birth experience by putting their faith in Jesus. It is impossible because in our natural fallen state, we cannot contain the things of God.

"But the natural man receiveth not the things of the Spirit of God: for they are foolishness unto him: neither can he know them, because they are spiritually discerned."

1 Corinthians 2:14

Whereas in the world, "seeing is believing," with the things of God, believing comes first. We must first believe in Jesus, accept that He has provided for us new life in the spirit and put our faith and trust in His finished work. Only then are we ready to receive the gift of the Comforter. With a regenerated spirit in place, the Holy Spirit can guide the believer into a continuous experience of the power and the presence of God.

Jesus appeared to His disciples on the day of His resurrection. It was evening, and they were shut in for fear of persecution. Despite the doors being securely locked, Jesus appeared in the midst of them. They were overjoyed to see Him. He was now the resurrected Christ and it was the moment that He would share the miracle of His resurrection with them.

"... He breathed on them and said to them, 'Receive the Holy Spirit.'"

John 20:22 NASB

Mankind, who had been in the shadows ever since the fall, was now receiving from the Creator of the universe, the ability to breathe again. They were once dead in their trespasses. Now they have risen together with Him.[7] The disciples had securely placed their faith in Jesus as the Son of God. Humanity registered brightly once again on heaven's radar. Except now, when the Father looks down from heaven to look at one of his children, He sees Jesus. As the second Adam, Jesus did not just restore what was lost to Adam. He offered humanity a place far above what Adam ever had.

"Even when we were dead in sins, hath quickened us together with Christ, (by grace ye are saved;)

And hath raised us up together, and made us sit together in heavenly places in Christ Jesus"

Ephesians 2:5-6

As believers, we are now seated in heavenly places in Christ. God's grace far exceeded Adam's sin.

All that Jesus would inherit as the Son of God would now be made available to His disciples and to all who would come to believe in Him through their testimony. They were now positioned to experience the connection Jesus enjoyed with the Father. When Christ resurrected bodily, they also did, in spirit. It was a deposit of a bodily resurrection to follow, at Jesus' second coming. They now possessed the adequate vessels in which God would pour the Holy Spirit. Now they were ready to experience the new reality that would come at the outpouring 40 days later. They were now ready to "receive the Holy Spirit."

Notes

1. Genesis 1:27-28

2. Luke 22:49

3. John 20:9

4. Matthew 1:18

5. John 7:37-38

6. John 10:9-16

7. Ephesians 2:1; Colossians 2:13; 1 Timothy 5:6

New wineskins represent the new birth experience.

***

"...He breathed on them and said to them, "Receive the Holy Spirit.""

John 20:22 NKJV

"It is not just sufficient for God to deliver His people. He wants to make a show of it as He provides them the comfort they need to recover and restore them to a place of destiny. He wants to be demonstrative of His work of delivering from spiritual oppression on this side of eternity; in the physical."

Chapter 4

COMFORT FROM THE INSIDE OUT

*Comfort, comfort my people, says your God. Speak tenderly to
Jerusalem, and proclaim to her that her hard service has been
completed, that her sin has been paid for, that she has received from
the Lord's hand double for all her sins*

Isaiah 40:1-2 NIV

When we are first introduced to the Holy Spirit in the book
of Genesis, He is described as hovering over the earth.[1]
We soon see Him striving with the wicked generation
of Noah's time.[2] We then see Him come upon Samson, empowering
him to perform his legendary strongman feats. Under His influence
other judges and prophets perform exploits and prophesy. In most
of these instances, the Holy Spirit is mentioned in passing. He is
most prominently mentioned in the Old Testament, however,
prophetically as one who would be given as a Promised Gift. When
Jesus was relating the Comforter's promise to His disciples, He was
reiterating the promise the heavenly Father made to the prophets
in separate instances in the past. These promises are found in the
old testament and speak of a momentous one-time event when this
precious gift would be dispensed.[3] We have come to recognize this

event as the outpouring of The Holy Spirit, which occurred on the day of Pentecost, 10 days after Jesus ascended to be with the Father. That fateful day marked a cataclysmic shift in the spirit realm that would have far-reaching consequences in how each believer can experience God.

The Jewish festival known in Hebrew as *Shavuot* commemorated the day Moses presented covenant law to the children of Israel on Mount Sinai. In Ancient Greek, this holiday was called "Pentecost" (literally "fiftieth day") because it came 50 days after the Passover. It seems fitting that on a day set to commemorate the old Covenant, God would pour out His Holy Spirit to put into place a new one:

"Behold, the days are coming, says the Lord, when I will make a new covenant with the house of Israel and with the house of Judah— not according to the covenant that I made with their fathers in the day that I took them by the hand to lead them out of the land of Egypt, My covenant which they broke, though I was a husband to them, says the Lord. But this is the covenant that I will make with the house of Israel after those days, says the Lord: I will put My law in their minds, and write it on their hearts; and I will be their God, and they shall be My people. No more shall every man teach his neighbor, and every man his brother, saying, 'Know the Lord,' for they all shall know Me, from the least of them to the greatest of them, says the Lord. For I will forgive their iniquity, and their sin I will remember no more."

Jeremiah 31:31-34 NKJV

The old covenant was an agreement based on outward observances that the children of Israel were unable to keep. As a result, their religious leaders clung to the trappings and outward expressions of religious devotion. The new covenant would be an inner experience;

one marked by true power and divine transformation. The believers living under this dispensation of God's grace would experience, God in intimate ways never known to mankind before and do exploits never seen before.

Rather than merely coming "upon" them, as He did on the saints in the old testament, the Holy Spirit would now dwell within each believer. The believer's spirit is immersed in God's presence and made pliable to sustain and experience the continual filling and overflow of the Holy Spirit. Like Jesus foretold,

"...out of his belly will flow rivers of living waters."

John 7:38

Never before had mankind had such access to the heart of God. This shift occurred in the spirit realm at the resurrection of Christ. Before then, there is no mention in scriptures of the baptism and the subsequent indwelling of the Holy Spirit as an experience that was available to the believer.

The disciples that stood before the risen Lord the Sunday evening of His resurrection, stood as recipients of His sweeping act of deliverance. They represented an oppressed people on the cusp of freedom. On the one hand, they represented Israel's children because they were all Jews surviving under the iron fist of imperial Rome. On the other hand, they represented all of humanity that had floundered in the shadows under the oppression of sin. As Jesus breathed on them that evening, they crossed from death to life in the spirit. Their destinies were set for eternal life. The course of their journey had been changed. They would never be the same.

The story could have ended there. Jesus, having snatched the keys of death, Hades and the grave back from Satan, restored what was lost to Adam. He made salvation available to the disciples by taking on the penalty for sin. The disciples could now technically stand before the Heavenly Father righteous and acceptable had they ascended with Jesus. Why didn't the story end there?

The story of man's redemption could have ended with the sweeping and dramatic events surrounding the resurrection of Christ. The massive stone being rolled away and Jesus bursting out from the grip of death could have been the climactic and triumphal end to the saga. Were it the case, first of all, you and I wouldn't be around. In other words, God's plan during the dispensation of grace is to increase the number of His fold. He wishes that no one is lost, but for as many people as possible will receive salvation.[4] Secondly, in all the examples of deliverance in the scriptures, God has a process of restoration whereby He takes His people from the identity of being slaves and brings them into being sons and daughters. Ultimately, the Holy Spirit's internal work in His role of comforter creates and deepens a personal bond that each believer can experience with the Father.

The theme of God's deliverance was not new to the disciples. They were of an ethnic group that was very much acquainted with oppression. In fact, they had been preparing to celebrate the Passover with Jesus when the events leading to the crucifixion transpired. It is a holiday, that to this day is celebrated annually by Jews worldwide to commemorate the night that God delivered their ancestors from the oppression of Pharaoh in Egypt. The children of Israel were set aside as God's special people because it was promised to their forefathers, Abraham, Isaac and Jacob, that through their line, the Messiah would come to the world. God had made a covenant with them, but they struggled to remain faithful to God because of their sinful nature.

As a result, they were carried into captivity by foreign powers, where they would suffer oppression time and time again. For this reason, when the books of the prophets are read in the Old Testament, there is a strong theme of deliverance. The Lord is seen continuously in scripture beckoning His people:

"Awake, awake! Put on your strength, O Zion; Put on your beautiful garments, O Jerusalem, the holy city! For the uncircumcised and the unclean shall no longer come to you. Shake yourself from the dust, arise; Sit down, O Jerusalem! Lose yourself from the bonds of your neck, O captive daughter of Zion!"

Isaiah 52:1-2 NKJV

So, when the storms of life are raging, and it may seem like there is no way out...be encouraged. God's posture is always one of declaring deliverance to His Children. We are not supposed to mourn our past slavery in sackcloths and ashes. God wants us to experience ever-increasing levels of glory in our new identities as his sons and daughters.

Nevertheless, adjusting to a mindset of liberty after a lifetime under the yoke of bondage does not come without the need for assistance. Those living under the authority of an oppressor often long for deliverance. While under bondage, the thought of freedom seems to be the only thing needed to satisfy their hopes and dreams. What couldn't be accomplished if only they had freedom? They might seldom stop and think of what is on the other side of freedom: the need for healing, restoration and self-governance. Life after being delivered from oppression can present challenges that can stir up deep insecurities about the future and grief about the past. As Comforter, the Holy Spirit is there to provide guidance and leadership to the believers as they reclaim a divine destiny.

From Slaves to Sons and Daughters

The journey of discovering the God-ordained destiny for the believer can be similar to the experience that the children of Israel had when they were returning from exile to the battered ruins of Jerusalem. Once the light of the known world, they were far from Solomon's day and the splendor of the great temple. Once considered one of the wonders of the world, now it lay in ruins as a haunting reminder of their powerlessness in the face of the empires of the world. They were intended to have a great destiny, and here they were, faced with being crushed. They must have been overwhelmed by a sense of smallness. They were now at the edge of their future. They were free to build toward it. But in the rubble mass, what they first had to clean up was a confrontation of the reality they had just left. They hadn't been in Babylon vacationing. They didn't just go on holiday and decide to stay. They were exiled, forced to leave their homeland. Some of them dragged by hooks in their noses. There is no moving forward without picking up the pieces of the ravaged past. There is no rebuilding without first cleaning up the mess left from the trauma of the past. It is a reality that is daunting and discouraging. In that state of mind, the Lord reaches out to them to offer the only thing that will allow them to grip the hand of courage once more. He offers comfort:

"Comfort, comfort my people, says your God. Speak tenderly to Jerusalem, and proclaim to her that her hard service has been completed, that her sin has been paid for, that she has received from the Lord's hand double for all her sins."

Isaiah 40:1-2 NIV

What will comfort do in the face of the tremendous task at hand? The task of building a destiny. How many would rather it be some form of tangible material help? Reparations, a down payment, some building equipment, more hands for labor, perhaps. Why something so nebulous and apparently immaterial like "comfort"? You can't exactly take comfort to the bank. Yes, they were now free to rebuild. What on earth could stop them? Isn't redemption all they needed while in the grips of slavery? Salvation is enough. Is it not?

Fast forward some 400 years, and Jesus is standing before His disciples having "breathed" them into a new era.[5] They stood at the brink of destiny. The world as they had all known it was about to change. They were ready to receive the gift of the Comforter. They hoped Jesus would be crowned king. They were now standing in their freedom and deliverance from sin. Wouldn't they need a gift that would be more assertive, more tangible, more affirming and proactive than "comfort" from a Comforter? The word "comforter" is translated from the ancient Greek word paraklétos. It is also often translated as "aid" or "helper." It would be tempting to prefer this latter as a translation in this context. Especially if we are the self-assertive types upon having been delivered, the types to say "thank you God for saving me; now, I've got this!" After all, we certainly all could use some help from time to time. Upon receiving our salvation, we must not think we can go about attempting to live a godly life by our own effort. If we do, we will soon run into the trouble of our fallen human nature. Our flesh is not regenerated and is not saved, though our spirits might be. We soon encounter the fact that we still have to deal with the dust. The dust of our fallen make-up and the dust of the troubles of daily life. The Holy Spirit does indeed serve as an aid and helper. It is His role in the Godhead. He aids God the

Father, Jesus Christ the Son, and you and me. When translated "aid" or "helper," in the context of Jesus presenting Him as a gift to His followers, paraklétos might evoke an image of simple assistance. When translated as "comforter," however, this title for the Holy Spirit presupposes a condition of brokenness in the person who needs Him. In light of the believer's deliverance, it is vital that we come to know the Holy Spirit as indeed, the Comforter.

As a believer, how do you get past the pain of the past to take hold of your freedom? How do you clean up the rubble of the past as you build on the destiny God intended for you from before the foundation of the world? Redeemed people are often ravaged people who have come through pillage and heartache into a brighter day. When the euphoria of having received a proclamation of freedom passes. When the goose pimples and emotion of the salvation experience are in the past, those who have been through the struggle of oppression need comfort. It is through His comfort that the Glory of the Lord is revealed.

"And the glory of the Lord shall be revealed, and all flesh shall see it together: for the mouth of the Lord hath spoken it."

It is not just sufficient for God to deliver His people. He wants to make a show of it as He provides them the comfort they need to recover and restore them to a place of destiny. He wants to be demonstrative of His work of delivering them from spiritual oppression on this side of eternity; in the physical. All flesh, that is, all in the natural realm, will behold His glory. They will say, "there is no way that such a recovery can be accomplished save for the direct hand of God."

Recalling her spiritual journey, one believer said: "He truly comforts us; He truly does. I am so comforted to know that my present circumstance isn't all there is. He has a future for me, and that is comforting." As believers having come through the ravages of the sinful world and into the glorious light, we need comfort. Imagine all you know is bondage, pillage, hardship and one day you find that you are free. You are brought into the glorious light of opportunities.

On the one hand, you are thrilled of all that is possible that you could have never conceived to be attainable before. But on the other hand, you are overwhelmed with the grief of all you have missed out on during your bondage. You look back on all you have experienced in your ignorance and realize the depths of injustice you have come through. You had no true idea while you were in it. You might have only had an inclination that something wasn't right. Something in you begged for more. But now that you are free, you find yourself debilitated by indignation and grief for what the road has wrought. As believers as we look out at the landscape of our lives and see the ravages that sin has left behind, it may cause us to feel faint. Will I ever have victory over this sin in my life? Will I ever be free from this addiction? Am I truly forgiven? As you begin to follow the Lord, the present circumstances surrounding you may cause you to call in question your salvation. If I am saved, why do I still deal with health issues, financial trouble, pain from past relationships or other calamities? But the LORD's comfort affirms that the war is truly over you are indeed forgiven. The Holy Spirit is a Comforter to support you along the journey.

It is so easy to rail against the injustices in the world. When we see others oppressed, it eats at us. Even worse are those who do not know that they are being oppressed and go along with it. It's not just a cry for justice but for a deep level of restoration. It's not enough for the pain to just stop and for the bad guys to go to jail, but there is a desire that goes beyond justice. There is a call for restitution and restoration. There is something deep inside of us that longs for freedom, deliverance and comfort. Harriet Tubman said famously, "I could have freed more if only they knew they were slaves." For a Christian to come to Christ is a big accomplishment; they have crossed from death to life and escaped the penalty of sin. How many more can step into a brighter and richer freedom if they only knew there is more available. Like the slaves that refused to go with Harriet Tubman, many Christians shy away from the Holy Spirit and lead lives of oppression and heartache, never realizing their God-given potential. The constant comfort provided by the Holy Spirit will allow them to not only have victory in their lives but to lead lives of maximum impact.

It is through the internal work of comfort that the plan of God will be carried out. He plans to expand His dominion throughout the natural realm, one believing soul at a time. During His three-year ministry, Jesus announced His coming kingdom. His parables were word-pictures to give glimpses of what it would be like. These stories and illustrations could only give ideas of what the coming kingdom would be like because it would be something the listeners had never experienced before. So many of Jesus' stories began with "the kingdom is like..." Imagine you visited a very remote part of the earth where the inhabitants of this place have had absolutely no contact with the modern amenities of life. How would you explain running water, electricity or the internet? You would probably be confined to using the tools, materials and experiences in their environment as references. These examples would only give them a glimpse of a reality they've neither seen nor thought of before.

In addition to Jesus' teaching, the miracles and exploits He performed in His ministry were meant to serve as examples to His followers of what their spiritual experiences and capabilities would be like in the coming kingdom. What are the markers of life in the spirit? What experiences are available to the believer on this side of eternity? What does the kingdom of God look like from the vantage point of the believer's life?

First of all, His coming kingdom was not an experience reserved for the afterlife. Jesus was describing a reality that He would place firmly into the hands of His disciples:

"I will give you the keys of the kingdom of heaven; whatever you bind on earth will be bound in heaven, and whatever you loose on earth will be loosed in heaven."

Matthew 16:19, NIV

Secondly, Jesus promised His disciples that the same authority that He displayed over nature and the spirit realm would be made available to them in His name. At the resurrection, Jesus snatched the keys of death, hades and the grave from Satan's hands.[6] His triumph over the grave meant all that Adam lost due to the fall, would be restored to humanity at the outpouring of the Holy Spirit. After instructing them to wait in Jerusalem until the arrival of the Holy Spirit, His parting words to the disciples at His ascension were:

"...All authority has been given to Me in heaven and on earth. Go therefore and make disciples of all the nations, baptizing them in the name of the Father and the Son and the Holy Spirit"

Matthew 28:18-19, NASB

Thirdly, the signs and wonders that were the normal order of the day in Jesus' ministry while He walked the earth, would accompany the ministry of those who would believe in Him. This is a startling promise:

"And these signs shall follow them that believe; In my name shall they cast out devils; they shall speak with new tongues;

They shall take up serpents; and if they drink any deadly thing, it shall not hurt them; they shall lay hands on the sick, and they shall recover."
Mark 16:17-18

Imagine how astonished people must have been to observe His miracles at that time. People often get preoccupied with the desire to see signs and wonders. To Jesus, these were not the core purpose of His mission but something of a windfall effect. In fact, He denounces the preoccupation with signs and wonders.[7] Jesus seemed more intent on His followers accessing the means of all His phenomenal work, versus the glorying in its physical manifestation. By what means would phenomenal exploits be part of the normal experience of believers? To begin to answer that question let us examine by what means it was the experience of Jesus while He walked the earth. What was the source of Jesus' power and command over nature?

The authority Jesus had over nature came directly from God. He attributed his wondrous works to a connection to the Father, made possible by His being filled with the Holy Spirit. Jesus began His ministry at the age of 30 when He was baptized by John the Baptist. The Holy Spirit descended upon Him and remained on Him.[8] Before Jesus began to preach, He spent 40 days in the wilderness fasting and praying. It was the Holy Spirit that led Him into that time of acute connection with the Father. This occurred only after Jesus was baptized by John the Baptist, where The Holy Spirit commissioned Jesus and empowered Him to do ministry. He came back from the desert and announced the beginning of His ministry by reading a prophetic passage in a synagogue:

"The Spirit of the Lord is upon me, because he hath anointed me to preach the gospel to the poor; he hath sent me to heal the brokenhearted, to preach deliverance to the captives, and recovering of sight to the blind, to set at liberty them that are bruised,

To preach the acceptable year of the Lord.

And he closed the book, and he gave it again to the minister, and sat down. And the eyes of all them that were in the synagogue were fastened on him.

And he began to say unto them, This day is this scripture fulfilled in your ears."

Luke 4:18-21

During His ministry, Jesus assured the disciples that they would be able to perform greater exploits on the earth as well, through the intimate connection that the Holy Spirit would provide them to the Father.

"Verily, verily, I say unto you, He that believeth on me, the works that I do shall he do also; and greater works than these shall he do; because I go unto my Father."

John 14:12

An identity as a child of God is not one that comes about by simply being outwardly labeled. Rather, it comes from an internal abiding in God through faith.[9] God is in the business of performing the supernatural, not the superficial. Through the work of helping the believer navigate and overcome the storms and trials of life, the Holy Spirit cements the believer's identity as a child of God. He flips the script on suffering, if you will, by making it an agent of character building and spiritual development. Dust storms are no longer just a source of wanton pain. The disciples had been delivered from being slaves to fear and sin, to become the very sons and daughters of God.

The Holy Spirit gave them mighty power to proclaim the gospel to the lost. Their fear and cowardice turned into bold preaching on the day of Pentecost. As a result, thousands were added to the number of believers.

The Holy Spirit works internally in the work of healing us spiritually, much as a medical professional would do in the natural. As He goes to the root of spiritual afflictions to bring healing and victory to the believer's life. Subsequently, the process of His work produces trust and intimacy between the believer and the Heavenly Father.

Recently, a friend of mine told me about an irritation on his skin. As time passed, the irritation worsened. He attempted to heal himself with over-the-counter topical ointments. After spending much money and effort to deal with the problem himself, he decided to seek a professional. The doctor diagnosed him with shingles. It is caused by the chickenpox virus, which though he had when he was a child, lay dormant for most of his life. That is until it found an opportunity to resurface as shingles as a result of his weak immune system. This is much like how the Holy Spirit addresses sin in our lives. He seeks out the root, that may be derived from spiritual afflictions set in motion early in our journey, which lay dormant until an opportune moment of weakness is present. There might even be propensities toward sin that may be dormant as a result of things set in motion before our birth and outside of the influence of our personal choices:

"Surely I was sinful at birth, sinful from the time my mother conceived me."

Psalms 51:5 NIV

It might be devastating for a believer to realize that their struggle against being bent toward a particular kind of bondage might have come about of no choice of their own. In their desire to please the Lord and live a righteous life, they can be daunted by the struggle between their willing spirit and their helplessly weak flesh. The Holy Spirit works to heal the broken areas from the inside out to offer the believer true transformation and restoration versus a temporary and superficial fix. He administers comfort to the believer struggling with confronting spiritual viruses by bringing to memory God's word and reminding the believer of the grace that is available in the process of sanctification.

The Holy Spirit works as Comforter in the life of believers to deepen and personalize the bond we have with the Father. We get to know Him as Healer, Provider, Deliverer and Friend. His multifaceted work sets us about on the path of being more like the Father. Through what we are witnessing in our intimate lives and personal experiences, we are empowered and motivated to share God with others. We come to share His burden for freeing and saving the lost. We come to share His desire to create more life-saving and intimate connections with others. As the Holy Spirit works in us, we mature to a level of being empowered to carry out the mission to make more disciples allowing Him to save more souls.

"Again I looked and saw all the oppression that was taking place under the sun: I saw the tears of the oppressed and they have no comforter; power was on the side of their oppressors— and they have no comforter. And I declared that the dead, who had already died, are happier than the living, who are still alive."

Ecclesiastes 4:1-2 NIV

When Jesus was talking to His disciples in John 14:26, He called the Holy Spirit the "Comforter." One of the Holy Spirit's works in believers' lives is to provide comfort in moments of distress. This proves His gentleness toward us and the power to maintain our hope of faith. Subsequently, this empowers us to continue in the faith and the works of God despite tribulations that arise to discourage us from the hope of the Gospel. When we feel imperfect, discouraged or lost, the Comforter reminds us that we are still children of God. The Spirit bears witness with our spirits by assuring and reassuring that we are of God. He desires to heal and comfort from the inside out.

Notes

1. Genesis 1:2

2. Genesis 6:3

3. Zechariah 12:10; Joel 2:28; Isaiah 44:3

4. 2 Peter 3:9

5. John 20:22

6. Revelation 1:18

7. Matthew 16:4; 1 Corinthians 1:22-23

8. John 1:32-33

9. Romans 2:28-29

"The comfort the Holy Spirit provides during the struggles and storms of life serves to lead us to line up our priorities properly. A child of God is referenced to the Heavenly Father relationally. He comes first in time, resources and affection. God will often allow suffering into the lives of His children to help them set their priorities on the kingdom."

Chapter 5

SONSHIP THROUGH HARDSHIP

But we see Jesus, who was made a little lower than the angels for the suffering of death, crowned with glory and honour; that he by the grace of God should taste death for every man.

For it became him, for whom are all things, and by whom are all things, in bringing many sons unto glory, to make the captain of their salvation perfect through sufferings.

Hebrews 2:9-10

Salvation is Christ's thrilling accomplishment. The sinner condemned to death is gifted with life. That life is generally depicted as a promise of a life to come after death. So why doesn't the believer just die when he accepts this amazing gift?

Why didn't the story just end for all humanity once Jesus rose from the dead? Because the story doesn't end at salvation.

Jesus is the doorway into a reality that the believer is meant to experience while still alive on earth. The true "normal" experience of Christianity is one intended to be rich with the phenomenal movement of the Spirit of God. It is a life of continuously encountering the power and the presence of God.

That power becomes evident in the believer's life by acting not just to free the sinner from the penalty of death but also its power over daily life. As the believer comes to know the Holy Spirit as Comforter, another phenomenal thing takes place. The bond of trust that He nurtures between the believer and the Heavenly Father, as He teaches the believer to take on the identity of Christ and act in His name, solidifies the believer's adoption as a child of God.

Aren't all people children of God? There is a general hesitation to classify any particular group of people as being God's people versus others in today's politically correct society. Despite what the world might think, the Son of God is an exclusive title. Only Jesus holds it. As a result, only those who believe in His name can biblically be considered children of God.[1] This ability to receive the Holy Spirit was only made available through Jesus' suffering, death and resurrection. Life in the spirit is only accessible by a continual and abiding faith in Jesus' finished work. The Bible refers to the suffering of Jesus as the price He paid so that God the Father might have many sons and daughters.

But we see Jesus, who was made a little lower than the angels for the suffering of death, crowned with glory and honour; that he by the grace of God should taste death for every man.

For it became him, for whom are all things, and by whom are all things, in bringing many sons unto glory, to make the captain of their salvation perfect through sufferings.

Hebrews 2:9-10

It is through suffering that Jesus was able to extend the rights of His Sonship to those who believed in Him. No one knows the Father as intimately as His Son Jesus and vice versa. The bond of fellowship in the Godhead is what allows the presence and the power to flow. Likewise, through the suffering in life, we come to intimately know God through the work of the Holy Spirit.

To profess faith in Christ and yet not seek to be baptized and filled with the Holy Spirit is like being an orphan that takes hold of his adoption papers and changes his name and yet refuses to take hold of the rights and privileges of being a son. It is the believer who possesses the indwelling Spirit of God and is the one in the position to enjoy the rights and privileges of being adopted as a child of God. The manifestation of a fruitful life is, subsequently, the work of the Comforter's presence in a believer's life.

We naturally despise suffering. Our nature is to lean toward comfort and ease. When we realize the Holy Spirit uses seasons of suffering to advance us in our spiritual experience; we might begin to glory in them and look forward to the rewards of faithfully enduring them with His help. The Apostle Paul found his sufferings offered him a unique connection with Jesus. It caused him to identify with what Jesus went through. By comparison, even if only a little bit, he sensed an empathy for Christ while enduring his suffering. Soon, looking for that closeness to Christ that came as a result of the suffering it became the focal point of the Apostle Paul's spiritual ambitions:

"That I may know him, and the power of his resurrection, and the fellowship of his sufferings..."

Philippians 3:10

God doesn't intend that we be masochists. We don't have to look for suffering, nor do we have to stir up storms in life. They will come simply as a result of being in a fallen world. Through the presence of the Holy Spirit, we can count it all joy.[2] We can be certain that the sufferings don't come to inflict wanton pain, nor as punishment. Jesus bore the pain and suffering as punishment for your sins. For you to endure suffering as punishment would be double jeopardy. The crimes you have committed against heaven have been paid for by Him.

Surely he hath borne our griefs, and carried our sorrows: yet we did esteem him stricken, smitten of God, and afflicted.

But he was wounded for our transgressions, he was bruised for our iniquities: the chastisement of our peace was upon him; and with his stripes we are healed.

Isaiah 53:4-5

Therefore, for a believer, the sufferings and trials of life come exclusively to be used by the Holy Spirit to solidify our identity as children of God. Suffering does not earn us the position of children. It just creates a level of responsibility to allow God to trust us with the rights and privileges that come to us as His children. Jesus, Himself set this pattern in place, regarding suffering:

"Although He was a Son, He learned obedience from the things which He suffered."

Hebrews 5:8 NASB

In our personal walk, there are common ways that the Holy Spirit will use suffering and solidify our identity as children of God.

One of the aims of the Holy Spirit, as he comforts us through the trials of life, is by teaching us to be fixed forward in our gaze. The

Christian life is designed to be an onward and upward progression, from glory to glory. Have you ever experienced someone talking about the "old times," and the old times are long gone? It is similar to a 60-year-old talking like he is still 30 years old. Instead of embracing the present, they would prefer to live in the past. When we battle against the pruning process, we stir up the dust of the past, decayed and dead things in our life.

Consider the rearview mirror of your car. The average size is about eight to ten inches while the average length of your windshield is about 65 inches. Why? Drivers are supposed to glance behind them, not stare. Accordingly, our focus should be forward. In Genesis 19, the angels of the Lord told Lot to flee Sodom and Gomorrah.

"Then the LORD rained upon Sodom and upon Gomorrah brimstone and fire from the LORD out of heaven; And he overthrew those cities, and all the plain, and all the inhabitants of the cities, and that which grew upon the ground. But his wife looked back from behind him, and she became a pillar of salt."

Genesis 19:24-26

There is no grace or glory in living a life of constantly looking back. I believe when a woman looks back, she becomes bitter, and when a man looks back, he becomes dull. Whether it be nostalgia, the past has passed. Paul the Apostle said it best,

"Brethren, I count not myself to have apprehended: but this one thing I do, forgetting those things which are behind, and reaching forth unto those things which are before."

Philippians 3:13

You may take an occasional glance at the past but focus on the future. Hindsight plus foresight equal insight.

The comfort the Holy Spirit provides during the struggles and storms of life leads us to line up our priorities properly. A child of God is referenced to the Heavenly Father relationally. He comes first in time, resources, and affection. God will often allow suffering in His children's lives to help them set their priorities on the kingdom. Navigating through them with the help and comfort of the Holy Spirit, serves to remind us we are only passing through this life. We are not here to be held down by distractions. As ambassadors of the kingdom, we are on a mission and everything and everyone that occupies our lives must honor our mission.

What would you do if God removed certain people and things from your life? Since we see things and relationships as valuable, it is our nature to prioritize them before God. However, we must ensure that God is a priority and that we depend on Him. When God moved King Uzziah out of the way, Isaiah saw the Lord.[3]

Sometimes we allow relationships, good or bad, to have more dominance over our lives than they should. No man or woman should stand between you and God.

"Jesus said unto him, Thou shalt love the Lord thy God with all thy heart, and with all thy soul, and with all thy mind."

Matthew 22:37

No pain, issue or death can separate us from the love of God. Christ covers it all; your passion, emotions, treasure, values and intellect should be Christ-centered.

Life in the modern world can be marked by a preoccupation with material things. Nevertheless, everyone is faced with challenges. Whether you are rich or poor, storms do not discriminate. Jesus said,

"...one's life does not consist in the abundance of the things he possesses."

Luke 12:15 NJKV

Despite their abundance, some have succumbed to their storms due to frustration and hopelessness. God intends that no matter what our station might be in life, the Holy Spirit will be there to help us respond to the storms of life. Only His abiding and comforting presence can bring about the growth out of pain and trials common to human existence.

Sometimes growth is a byproduct of the storms and trials. Other times God allows them for the express purpose of pruning our lives. When a gardener prunes a vine, he cuts off the dead and wilted limbs. They hold up the plant's growth by taking up the nutrients that would be best used by the healthier parts of the plant. So, in the Christian walk, the process of pruning refers to God allowing the challenges and trials of life for the express purpose of removing the dead, dying and useless issues of our lives. These are issues that are just hanging on and hindering the efficiency of growth. The Lord uses pruning like a wise father that trains his children to be strong to overcome life's challenges.

"Blessed be the Lord my strength which teacheth my hands to war, and my fingers to fight."

Psalm 144:1

Clearly, this process does not exist to discourage us from following the Lord but to make us better as we follow Him. We are then better equipped to help and encourage others when their pruning season arises.

After undergoing the pruning process, a plant that had maybe gone years without bearing fruit can begin to flourish–life and vitality return. Likewise, sometimes dead issues can linger in the experience of believers. Unbeknownst to them, these dead issues can be sucking the life out of a normally joyful walk with the Lord. Painful situations might arise, but it might be just the pruning process, come to restore life.

Another way that the Holy Spirit solidifies our adoption is by using suffering to allow us to experience God's closeness. The Holy Spirit is more than the physical evidence we feel or see in the Christian church. He is more than goose pimples, shakes, shivers, and speaking in tongues. He is closer to us than we are to ourselves. If He lives in you, He is in your mind. He is closer to your soul than you are. He is closer to your spirit than you are. He is even closer than you are to your own body. There are things He knows that no one else knows and that you in your mind are not yet aware of. When you hear a prophetic word spoken by another believer and realize that it is confirmation of what the Holy Spirit has spoken to you personally, it creates a thrilling sense of closeness to God. When you have fed your mind with the word of God, by developing a habit of daily Bible study, The Holy Spirits brings to your remembrance the verses that pertain to your situation. In this act, He is administering comfort to you and allowing you to feel the closeness of knowing that God is intimately acquainted with your struggle.

One of the reasons we do not experience breakthroughs in many areas of life is because we struggle to yield to the Spirit. However, since He knows so much about us, we can pray and ask Him to help us understand ourselves. You can pray, "Holy Spirit, I need to know more about me. What is going on with me?" Then, He can guide you in areas you did not know about you. We can avoid many mistakes in life if we learn to listen to the voice of the Holy Spirit. So, it is imperative we understand how He operates. Amid the dark clouds of the storms in life, He works to illuminate a path forward for the believer.

He was present with the Father when you were created. He is keenly aware of the destiny that the Father deposited in your spirit. He acts as a searchlight for your soul. He illuminates scripture to you as you read, highlighting what is pertinent to your spiritual journey.

"Thy word is a lamp unto my feet, and a light unto my path."

Psalm 119:105

In conjunction with the Word of God, the Spirit is a guiding light for the path we are destined to pursue in life.

"Oh, send out Your light and Your truth! Let them lead me..."

Psalm 43:3 NKJV

The following are seven ways we can experience the guiding light of the Spirit during personal struggle:

1. Making Contact with the Holy Spirit

We initiate contact with the Spirit through prayer. Yet, contact is not maintained through the posture of prayer or repetitive sayings.

Instead, prayer must be a lifestyle not a routine. We must consistently and intentionally communicate with the Spirit to develop an intimate relationship with Him. It is the only way we can become familiar with His voice. He is a gentle spirit and will not impose. We must actively invite Him into our day and into any struggle we might be facing. Through prayer, we let Him in on the details of our struggles and give Him permission to intervene and use it for God's glory. Additionally, daily communion with Him increases our ability to discern His instruction for our lives.

2. Explore deeper realms of the Spirit

Now, this is not to encourage you to go out and become bizarre. Essentially, I am encouraging you to become intimate with the Holy Spirit within the realm of the Word of God. Beyond what most typically experience, there is a deeper realm of the Spirit and a deeper anointing. Even with good intentions, it is possible to adopt the spirit of religion by doing the same thing the same way because it is how you were taught. Yet, the Comforter is saying, "I want you to know me more for yourself." Although we should wholeheartedly embrace the miracles and strange phenomena, we shouldn't only expect to experience Him in the dramatic. Sometimes, He manifests as a still small voice.[4] There is always a greater level to experience in the Spirit. Personal struggles allow us to experience the word of God in new ways. For instance, we might be more inclined to seek out particular bible stories in scripture in the midst of our trial. They might come to mind by some form of suggestion, like hearing it in passing or what might feel like a nudge or a hunch. Examining these stories during difficult times in our lives gives the Holy Spirit access to our minds to highlight keys inherent in the stories. The characters you might have encountered in the routine study can truly come alive when you are going through suffering similar to theirs. Stories

SONSHIP THROUGH HARDSHIP | 73

of the saints that may have gone through greater suffering, will put your plight into perspective. The Holy Spirit will point out things the characters felt or did. He might also highlight how God delivered or comforted them. He does so to comfort and encourage you in your journey.

3. Inspire others

God does not want us only to inspire others by our words. In addition, He wants us to accomplish something great for others to witness. When you are going through a trial, someone is always watching. You never know who you might inspire by coming through successfully. Sometimes it is the struggles of life that set up the platform for us to achieve great success.

"Very truly I tell you, whoever believes in me will do the works I have been doing, and they will do even greater things than these, because I am going to the Father."

John 14:12, NKJV

Achieving greatness serves as an example to others about the magnitude of the power of God. When we inspire others to become better, then we are truly operating as the body of Christ.

4. Seek personal revelation

Struggles often lead a believer to seek God in a personal way. Intently seeking Him brings the believer into a place of illumination. Illumination is the first stage of revelation; it is the prerequisite. The Word of God can be complex to the human mind. Revelation cannot be achieved through normal human understanding. God reveals insights into His word as we develop our personal bond with Him.

The Bible declares,

"For my thoughts are not your thoughts, neither are your ways my ways, declares the Lord. As the heavens are higher than the earth, so are my ways higher than your ways and my thoughts than your thoughts."

Isaiah 55:8-9 NIV

Consequently, the Holy Spirit must illuminate the Word for clarity and comprehension.

5. Invest in others

In the midst of our struggles, it is so easy to be preoccupied with ourselves. Do not be surprised if you find yourself prompted by the Holy Spirit , and He wants us to invest in others during this time. He is keenly interested in where we place our time, talent, and treasure. He might lead you to donate your resources to ministries, charities and organizations. He might also lead you to invest your time in people through mentoring, volunteering, and encouragement. It may sound counterintuitive to focus on others in times of your trials and struggles. But as the Comforter, He brings blessing and healing by inviting you to be part of His work. You can bless others from the vantage point of having been blessed yourself.

"Praise be to the God and Father of our Lord Jesus Christ, the Father of compassion and the God of all comfort, who comforts us in all our troubles, so that we can comfort those in any trouble with the comfort we ourselves receive from God. For just as we share abundantly in the sufferings of Christ, so also our comfort abounds through Christ."

2 Corinthians 1:3-5 NIV

In 1999, someone gave me a vehicle. Then, I turned around and gave it to a teenage boy. Today, that same young man has a strong career, two homes, a nice car, a wife and two children. It seems his ability to succeed exploded at once. However, in 1999, he was a brokenhearted young man. So, when the car was given to me, I fixed it and gave it to him instead of selling it. I signed the car over to him, gave him the keys and encouraged him to endure. Then, I trusted him with the car. And guess what? He grew. That car was fertilizer for his life; it was an investment.

6. Return to your first love experience with God

When the storms of life present themselves, hide yourself in the first love experience you had with God. Bring to mind what it was like when you were first saved and ask for a renewal of that passion you felt for God. Examine your life for evidence of idolatry. It could be that the trials you are currently experiencing have risen as a result of falling out of love with God. Only He can satisfy the longings of the soul. If you neglect your first love, your spirit will seek satisfaction in vain and pointless pursuits. The result is always pain and distraction. If you have allowed your spirit to become connected to people, things or material possessions that God did not design for you to connect, get rid of them. Drifting away from the Holy Spirit permits the opportunity for idol worship. Remember, the Comforter is your aid. He knows what the Father has planned for your life; He helps you along your spiritual journey.

Furthermore, do not allow others or possessions to become your primary love or focus of your worship.

"Nevertheless I have this against you, that you have left your first love."

Revelation 2:4 NKJV

This is the root of idolatry. If you search your heart and discover your treasure lies elsewhere, the Comforter can guide you back to the Father.

"For where your treasure is, there your heart will be also."

Matthew 6:21 NKJV

"...and do the things you did at first. If you do not repent, I will come to you and remove your lampstand from its place."

Revelation 2:5 NIV

Sometimes we accuse the devil of stealing our light. Yet, God says He will remove our light when we do not repent and return to Him— our first love. Similar to a romantic relationship, you must keep the fire burning to maintain love and intimacy. In fact, the burning is key to illumination.

7. Repent quickly

Not all struggles arise as a direct consequence of sin in our lives, but some do. When facing hardship, ask the Holy Spirit to help you examine your life to uncover any sin. Then quickly repent. Get in the habit of repenting quickly. When you refuse to confess your sins, you are easily entangled by self-righteousness. Confess your sin and quickly turn in the direction that God intends for you to go. Do not linger in self-condemnation. Doing so will open avenues for personal illness. Instead, choose a trustworthy brother or sister in the Lord and confess your sins, pray and move on in your journey with God.[5]"Consider how far you have fallen! Repent..." When you fall, consider the distance it creates between you and the Spirit and repent.

God has made provision for our journey here on earth. It is meant to be full of purpose. It is comforting and empowering to know that the struggles and storms we might encounter as believers are made to serve a purpose and accomplish the desired end. They are meant to solidify our identity as sons and daughters of God. It isn't just a nice label. We are seated in heavenly places with Christ, a position of power, dominion, and privilege.[6]

Notes

1. John 1:12-14

2. James 1:2-4

3. Isaiah 6:1

4. 1 Kings 19:11-13

5. James 5:16

6. Ephesians 1:3-6

"The Greek word translated as "comforter" when referring to the Holy Spirit is also translated as "advocate." It is defined as someone who is summoned to plead another's cause before a judge. We can envision Him by our side as we receive a verdict on our sin. He helps us to understand where we have gone wrong by making the scripture clear to us."

Chapter 6

A CLOSER LOOK AT THE HOLY SPIRIT

"If ye then, being evil, know how to give good gifts unto your children: How much more shall your heavenly Father give the Holy Spirit to them that ask him?" Luke 11:13

I t seemed like such a random act. The temple area must have been full of people. The Feast of Tabernacles drew a crowd of pilgrims every year to Jerusalem. All of a sudden, a voice thundered from the midst of the crowd:

"If any man thirst let Him come to me and drink!" It was Jesus. "Out of his belly shall flow rivers of living water," He continued. He was very deliberate and specific in His invitation. Still, the people didn't know because, he spoke of a future event according to the gospel account. Jesus was announcing the promise of the outpouring of the Holy Spirit, which would come on the day of Pentecost.

"But this spake he of the Spirit, which they that believe on him should receive for the Holy Ghost was not yet given; because that Jesus was not yet glorified."

John 7:39

John the Baptist, when foretelling of the ministry of Jesus, said,

"I baptize you with water for repentance. But after me comes one who is more powerful than I, whose sandals I am not worthy to carry. He will baptize you with the Holy Spirit and fire."

Matthew 3:11, NIV

Jesus was proclaiming to the crowd and to all humanity what He, himself, intended to do. Whereas John the Baptist was called a baptizer (or immerser) for his tendency to immerse people in the river Jordan, Jesus would be the ultimate immerser because He would baptize the believer in the fiery presence of the living God.[1] What would it be like to be baptized with the Holy Ghost and with fire?[2] Can you imagine the curiosity of those in attendance that day? "How can rivers flow from one's belly," they must have pondered. Have you ever wondered what it is like to encounter the Holy Spirit?

Jesus was giving an illustration of a life overflowing with the indwelling presence of God. John's reference to fire points to God's power. Both are vivid images that evoke wonder and intrigue. How do such experiences translate practically into the life of a believer? What does a life filled with the Holy Spirit look like? How will you know if you have been baptized or filled?

Every believer can benefit from taking a closer look at the Holy Spirit. Discovering more about Him enables us to know and experience Him on a deeper level. He is not a power we inherit at birth. He is a gift given by God.

A gift must be received, valued and cared for, and enjoyed to the fullest. In the modern-day, there can be many assumptions and false information to wade through when seeking clarity on the Holy Spirit. There is no safer option than examining scripture, with a heart set in faith in the person of Jesus. When you put your faith in Him, your spirit, which was once dead because of sin, is made alive and activated.[3] This allows you now to be a spiritual being. Only spiritual beings can understand spiritual things.[4] This is why Jesus is seen in the gospel accounts, repeatedly saying to people, "Come to me..." We must first come to Him for true understanding. He doesn't point to a set of instructions or to a recipe or formula. He points to Himself time and time again. The following are a few examples:

"I am the way the truth and the life, no one comes to the Father except through me."

John 14:6 NIV

"I am the door. If anyone enters by me, he will be saved, and go in and out and find pasture."

John 10:9

"I am the resurrection and the life..."

John 11:25

"Verily, Verily, I say unto you, Before Abraham was, I am."

John 8:58

Every prophet that came before Jesus would preface their utterances with the phrase "thus says the LORD" to loan credence to their declarations. They had to announce that they were speaking God's words. On the contrary, the declarations of Jesus would often begin with "Verily, verily I say to you..." [emphasis added]. Jesus spoke with divine authority. His tendency to do so enraged the religious rulers of the day and was part of the reason they plotted to assassinate Him.

Nevertheless, Jesus was intent on providing salvation so that with a resurrected spirit, the believer can bear witness of the Holy Spirit.[5] So you ask, how is it that you will know when the Holy Spirit is moving in your life. If you have come to Jesus and received salvation, your spirit and conscience will bear witness to the presence of the Spirit in your life.

Once you trust Him with your desire for the Holy Spirit, Jesus will make every provision to ensure you personally experience Him. This is why:

" *'I will be found by you,' declares the LORD, 'and will bring you back from captivity'..."*

Jeremiah 29:14 NIV

He wants you to find Him, and He promises that you will when you seek Him with all of your heart.[6] If you wish to encounter the Holy Spirit, you can pray the prayer, "Lord, please give me a burning desire to know you." God will begin to line up the circumstances in your life that will lead to your Holy Spirit baptism.

In the scriptures, we see examples of people receiving the Holy Spirit. Paul laid hands on believers who hadn't yet received the Holy Spirit, and their baptism ensued.[7] Follow the patterns spelled out in the scripture. Seek God in prayer. But also seek an elder who can lay hands on you and pray that you receive the Holy Spirit.

"And I say unto you, Ask, and it shall be given to you; seek, and ye shall find; knock, and it shall be opened unto you."

Luke 11:9

Jesus gave these instructions referring specifically to asking for the Holy Spirit. He says later in the same passage:

"If ye then, being evil, know how to give good gifts unto your children: How much more shall your heavenly Father give the Holy Spirit to them that ask him?"

Luke 11:13

When you ask God for the Holy Spirit, if you have accepted your adoption as His child by first having put faith in Jesus, there is no way you will be refused!

There is no room for complacency in your walk with God. If you are to take hold of all that God has for you to experience with Him, you must be willing to respond to every invitation to actively seek more of Him. He is a rewarder of those that diligently seek Him.[8]

Some people choose to focus on the fact that the scriptural accounts of believers receiving the Holy Spirit depicted them as having spoken in tongues. They create doctrines based on surrounding the outward expressions that accompanied a work or move of the Spirit at any given point. People who become overly concerned with the outward expression of these gifts can fall into the trap of religiosity. That is a concern with just the demonstration of religious life and a subsequent detachment from the spirit of why these visible things exist. Ever encounter a professed believer who can rattle off in "tongues" but refuses to speak to a neighbor or a brother or sister in Christ? They speak God in heavenly languages yet refuse to speak to fellow Christians in plain English. It would serve them to be reminded of what Jesus Himself said would be the indicator of a true believer:

"As I have loved you, so you must love one another. By this everyone will know that you are my disciples, if you love one another."

John 13:34-35 NIV

True believers are identified by their love for one another. So, if the Spirit resides within, you will be able to love even when it is difficult. Whereas tongues, prophesying and words of knowledge are gifts of the Spirit, love is paramount because it is a fruit of the Spirit. Although believers are admonished to desire spiritual gifts, the emphasis of the Christian faith is on earnestly pursuing love. [9]

The Apostle Paul must have dealt with this tendency in church culture because He wrote to address the issue saying:

"If I speak in the tongues of men or of angels, but do not have love, I am only a resounding gong or a clanging cymbal. If I have the gift of prophecy and can fathom all mysteries and all knowledge, and if I have a faith that can move mountains, but do not have love, I am nothing."

1 Corinthians 13:1-3 NIV

Rather than seeking out the gifts of the Spirit, focus intently on cultivating the fruit of the Spirit:

"But the fruit of the Spirit is love, joy, peace, forbearance, kindness, goodness, faithfulness, gentleness and self-control."

Galatians 5:22-23 NIV

The life of a believer is one of cultivation and bearing fruit. It's no wonder God set man in a garden when He first created Him. He wishes that we be fruitful and multiply. Love is the greatest fruit and the product of the inner-working of the Spirit.

God is a God of abundance. That is why God is the ultimate gift giver. He is in the business of lavishing His children with gifts upon more gifts. The Holy Spirit in His occupation as Comforter operates as the Gift that administers gifts to the believer. There are general gifts that all believers can experience personally, and there are specific gifts for the edification of the church that He assigns to whom He wills. He gives the manifestations of wondrous works such as miracles, prophecies and gifts of the Spirit to comfort and guide the church, especially in times where it may experience growing pains.

"There are diversities of gifts, but the same Spirit. There are differences of ministries, but the same Lord. And there are diversities of activities, but it is the same God who works all in all. But the manifestation of the Spirit is given to each one for the profit of all: for to one is given the word of wisdom through the Spirit, to another the word of knowledge through the same Spirit, to another faith by the same Spirit, to another gifts of healings by the same Spirit, to another the working of miracles, to another prophecy, to another discerning of spirits, to another different kinds of tongues, to another the interpretation of tongues. But one and the same Spirit works all these things, distributing to each one individually as He wills."

1 Corinthians 12:4-11, NKJV

The Holy Spirit is available to assist in all areas of spiritual cultivation needed to produce good fruit in the life of a believer. He begins by creating the environment for an encounter with God. No one can come to God unless they are drawn.[10] His first area of work is that of drawing sinners to repentance. The Holy Spirit nudges the conscience of those who are searching for God. Saul of Tarsus persecuted the early believers until He encountered Jesus on the road to the city of

Damascus and was converted. During the dramatic encounter with Christ that led to Saul's conversion, Jesus said to Saul, "it is hard for you to kick against the pricks." Some scholars attribute the phrase to agricultural origins, as in a device with pricks used to steer oxen. It would seem that Saul's conscience was pricking him for some time before he met Jesus personally. He was fighting his conscience in his religious zeal to exterminate early believers in Jesus. Later he went on to be known as Paul the Apostle and said the following:

"I tell the truth in Christ, I am not lying, my conscience also bearing me witness in the Holy Spirit, that I have great sorrow and continual grief in my heart. For I could wish that I myself were accursed from Christ for my brethren, my countrymen according to the flesh..."

Romans 9:1-3 NKJV

He who once hunted Christians because of their faith in Jesus now longed that those of his former religion would come to know and follow Jesus. His conscience had come a long way. On the way to Damascus to carry out his horrible errand, Saul's conscience contended with him because it bore witness to the Holy Spirit. As Paul the Apostle, he learned to listen to his conscience as an authority because he recognized that it bore witness to the Holy Spirit. The Holy Spirit works on the conscience of individuals to lead them to repentance. Therefore, the conscience serves as a witness to the presence of the Holy Spirit and becomes a powerful ally to the believer once it is nurtured and trained to respond to the sensitive leading of the Holy Spirit.

Another way the Holy Spirit leads individuals to repentance is by creating an atmosphere conducive to repentance. On the day of

Pentecost, thousands were added to the fold at the preaching of Peter.[11] The Holy Spirit was present. He created an atmosphere for the word of God to be delivered with power and might. That same atmosphere softened the hearts of the listeners because they responded the following way:

"Now when they heard this, they were cut to the heart, and said to Peter and the rest of the apostles, Men and brethren, what shall we do?"

Acts 2:37 NKJV

The Holy Spirit ministered to each person that was in attendance in a very special way by convicting them of sin. This act made way for them to accept God's gift of repentance.

Picture this: The gavel comes down on the striking block. The judge calls the courtroom to order. The accused is ordered to stand, accompanied by his counsel. Though standing, he is proverbially at the edge of his seat. His life's destiny hangs in the balance. The head juror reads the verdict— "Guilty!"

He has just been convicted. This is usually not a happy or desired outcome for anyone who has had to stand trial. In the same sentence that Jesus presented the Comforter as a gift to His followers, He announced that His first order of duty is to convict them of sin.[12] No one would like to get a guilty verdict. Even if you did do it (that is, commit the act of which you are accused), you might hope to get off on some technicality or based on a very good excuse. It's human nature. We all like to think deep down we are made of good stuff, even when we commit evil acts. It's called self-righteousness, and yes, it's a sin. How wicked can the human heart be? The Bible says it is "desperately" so and "deceitful above all things."[13] That is, your heart will fool you into thinking that you are doing the right thing even when your sin might seem obvious to others. Have you ever come across people committing pretty egregiously immoral acts, and yet they seem to carry on unfazed as if what they are doing is normal? You might think, how can they possibly be okay with such an arrangement. First of all, the devil is a liar and the father of lies. Secondly, a sinful heart always justifies wrong behavior along a gradient of relativism. Third, media outlets bombard the mind and imagination with immoral standards of living and present sin as desirable. The kingdom of darkness has its triune entity comprised of Satan (and his minions), the world, and the flesh. The devil's axis of evil. The human soul would not stand a chance save for the grace of God.

"Or do you think lightly of the riches of His kindness and tolerance and patience, not knowing that the kindness of God leads you to repentance?"

Romans 2:4 NASB

When God doles out His kindness, He includes repentance in the list of benefits that He makes available to His children. Repentance can only come after a conviction. Conviction doesn't feel good. To hear a legal declaration of your guilt might be a jarring experience. But for a believer, conviction is not equivalent to condemnation. The Bible says there is no condemnation for those who are in Christ.[14] Repentance is the gift that replaces condemnation. It is the opportunity to accept that Christ has taken the condemnation on your behalf. In legal terms, a conviction would be equivalent to receiving and agreeing with the verdict. Condemnation would be receiving a sentence or punishment. Rather than receive the punishment for sin, the believer receives the gift made available only by Christ's substitutionary sacrifice. Rather than walk toward the death penalty, the believer can take hold of the gift of Jesus, accepting guilt for the crime. They can turn in the opposite direction and, instead, walk toward life and liberty.

The Greek word translated as "comforter" when referring to the Holy Spirit is also translated as "advocate." It is defined as someone who is summoned to plead another's cause before a judge. We can envision Him by our side as we receive a verdict on our sin. He helps us to understand where we have gone wrong by making the scripture clear to us. The feeling of remorse that fills a believer when under conviction is a direct result of the Holy Spirit's work. He is the one who convicts. He convicts us and at the same time, provides comfort by assuring us that we can trust our fate to Christ.

When the Holy Spirit is present, He makes repentance available to the believer. Repentance is not something that one can just conjure up by simply admitting guilt.

When referred to in scripture it is, in many instances, presented as being granted by God. The following are some examples:

"He is the one whom God exalted to His right hand as a Prince and a Savior, to grant repentance to Israel, and forgiveness of sins."

Acts 5:31 NASB

"When they heard this, they quieted down and glorified God, saying, 'Well then, God has granted to the Gentiles also the repentance that leads to life'."

Acts 11:18 NASB

"...with gentleness correcting those who are in opposition, if perhaps God may grant them repentance leading to the knowledge of the truth..."

2 Timothy 2:25 NASB

The experience of repentance is not a one-time event in the life of a believer. It is a continuous experience that is encountered as the believer ascends to new heights in God. As the believer develops the habit of studying the word of God, the Holy Spirit uses it as an engine to influence repentance. The scripture compares the word to both a hammer and a fire; one to break and the other to melt the heart.

"Is not My word like a fire? says the Lord, And like a hammer that breaks the rock in pieces?"

Jeremiah 23:29 NKJV

The process is designed to make the heart malleable and moldable to the presence of God. It can feel uncomfortable, but His goal is to be a blessing and to have the Word applied to our lives. Every time we hear the Word is an opportunity to repent.

"For the word of God is quick, and powerful, and sharper than any two edged sword, piercing even to the dividing asunder of soul and spirit, and of the joints and marrow, and is a discerner of the thoughts and intents of the heart."

Hebrews 4:12

A hammer? A furnace? A double-edged sword? These all sound like tools to inflict pain. Though painful, these are all tools that the Holy Spirit uses to cultivate the believer's soul. It reminds me of the method of cultivation called "slash and burn" or fire-fallow cultivation, designed to create land suitable for growing. These images might conjure up the thought of pain, but the ultimate purpose is to create an environment that is suitable to yield good fruit. It might seem counter indicative to think of the Holy Spirit wielding a hammer and at the same time serving as a comforter. However, the process of bringing conviction to our hearts through the word of God goes hand in hand with providing comfort for the very sorrow He brings through convicting the heart of sin:

"Godly sorrow brings repentance that leads to salvation..."

2 Corinthians 7:10 NIV

Another way the Holy Spirit works in the believer to produce good fruit is by preparing their hearts as soil for God's word.

"Sow to yourselves in righteousness, reap in mercy; break up your fallow ground: for it is time to seek the Lord, till he come and rain righteousness upon you."

Hosea 10:12

The heart is the soil in which to cultivate the fruit of the Spirit. Envision the Holy Spirit as the one who is cultivating us to bear good fruit. Fallow ground is land that has been left idle and overgrown with weeds. It is not ready to receive the seeds. If a planter were to throw seed on that type of ground, it would have no effects. Jesus illustrates this in the parable of the sower:

"...A farmer went out to sow his seed. As he was scattering the seed, some fell along the path, and the birds came and ate it up. Some fell on rocky places, where it did not have much soil. It sprang up quickly, because the soil was shallow. But when the sun came up, the plants were scorched, and they withered because they had no

root. Other seed fell among thorns, which grew up and choked the plants. Still other seed fell on good soil, where it produced a crop—a hundred, sixty or thirty times what was sown. Whoever has ears, let them hear."

Matthew 13:3-9, NIV

The condition of the soil determines how well the seed will penetrate and if it will ever have a chance to germinate. This is the reason why two people can hear the very same word and have entirely different reactions. One might hear the word and be moved to tears, while the other not be fazed at all; no more moved by it than a deaf man to music. Some can get better, while others become still worse. The difference in the outcome is due to the disposition of the heart of the hearer of the word. The Holy Spirit prepares the heart to bear good fruit by creating conditions to make the heart receptive to God.

The different parts of cultivation are used throughout scripture in many interchangeable ways to explain spiritual development. No one element or component fits as an exact parallel to what happens in the spirit realm. It is a mystery much like the bible describes the mystery of the mechanisms of how a child develops in the womb:

"As you do not know the path of the wind, or how the body is formed in a mother's womb, so you cannot understand the work of God, the Maker of all things."

Ecclesiastes 11:5 NIV

Metaphors and similes of nature only serve to give us glimpses into what the process will be. We can only know what it is truly like by undertaking the journey of spiritual growth. Likewise, similes and metaphors are prevalent in scripture to explain the Holy Spirit. We can only truly know Him by experiencing Him for ourselves as we let Him work in our lives. The following are some examples of metaphors and similes that are used to give glimpses of the Comforter:

He is like the wind (John 3:8). We don't know exactly how He moves and we can't predict His actions, but we can perceive the effects of His presence.

The outpouring of the Holy Spirit is called the latter rain (Joel 2:23). He comes down from Heaven. He brings life and refreshing to the spiritual journey.

He is like rivers of living water (John 7:8). Rivers are a means of transport carrying in desired blessings and carrying out waste and undesirable traits. Rivers are for trade and commerce. Water washes and cleanses. Water transports nourishment to a fledgling seed to help it to grow.

When we have our hearts set on the intention of growing spiritually in a desire to know God more intimately, we become receptive to how God's Word presents the Holy Spirit. We begin to recognize His movement into our lives and receive confirmation from the testimonies of other believers. We begin to know Him better, and as a result, we grow to trust Him more.

<u>Notes</u>

1. Hebrews 12:29

2. Matthew 3:11

3. Ephesians 2:1

4. 1 Corinthians 2:14

5. Romans 8:18; 9:1

6. Jeremiah 29:13

7. Acts 19:6

8. Hebrews 11:6

9. 1 Corinthians 14:1

10. John 6:44; John 6:65

11. Acts 2:14-47

12. John 16:7-8

13. Jeremiah 17:9

14. Romans 8:1

Every believer can benefit from taking
a closer look at the Holy Spirit.

***

"And I will pour out on the house of David and the inhabitants of Jerusalem a Spirit of grace and supplication."

Zechariah 12:10 NIV

"The Christian can have peace in facing life's greatest challenge because Jesus defeated, death, hades and the grave. The Holy Spirit is constantly there to remind the believer of that victory in Jesus. The fact that the Holy Spirit is residing inside the believer serves as a guarantee of things to come because it took a miracle for it to happen."

Chapter 7

HIS COMFORT ON EVERY SIDE:
EXPERIENCING THE HOLY SPIRIT

"Thou shalt increase my greatness, and comfort me on every side."

Psalm 71:21

A rare antique painting is discovered. It has gone missing for so long that it is not even listed in the repertoire of works by the artist. Who knows how it ended up in the shadows. Maybe it was stolen by someone hoping to cash in at a later date only to be forgotten in the dark corner of someone's attic. It is the kind of scenario that fans of the TV show "Antique Roadshow" would love. Imagine discovering that a painting that has been sitting in your possession turns out to be worth millions. Upon coming across a piece of old art, you would only hope that its author would be a famous master artist from the distant past. If for some reason, it had not been signed by the author, experts would be brought in to observe the details of the painting to compare it to the existing paintings attributed to the artist. The fine lines made on the canvas due to the way the artist would apply strokes of paint would be compared. His fingerprint might be present as a result of manually blotting or blending the color. His use of light will be observed. Ultimately, an endless list of details will be compared to assess whether the mystery painting is indeed that of the famous artist. The details point to the author's technique and style.

In scripture, we are described as God's handiwork. He is shown as molding our characters as the potter molds clay. He, too, has a style and technique that is evident in the way He works to create a showpiece of our lives.

"For we are God's handiwork, created in Christ Jesus to do good works, which God prepared in advance for us to do."

Ephesians 2:10 NIV

The indwelling presence of the Holy Spirit in the life of a believer is the gift of God by whom He keeps giving. The work the Holy Spirit accomplishes in our lives by molding and shaping us, He does as Comforter. Comfort is His style of administering the gifts of God.

When a believer is convicted of sin, it can be a harrowing experience. There is remorse because, as a child of God, the spirit is inclined to please the Father. It can be heartbreaking to realize at new levels, time and time again, how easy it is to fall short. Falling into sin can cause you to question your standing with God and to feel like you are not His child. The Comforter is there to provide reassurance of God's grace and abiding favor.

"In whom ye also trusted, after that ye heard the word of truth, the gospel of your salvation: in whom also after that ye believed, ye were sealed with that holy Spirit of promise"

Ephesians 1:13

A seal carries the identity, authority and jurisdiction of kingship or dominion. God placed His identity upon us when He gave us the Holy Spirit. The Holy Spirit's presence in our lives is a reassurance that we indeed are His children and are not rejected when we fall short. He teaches and instructs as part of the process of bringing conviction and comforting the believer as He administers the gift of repentance. He brings to mind the scripture that offers reassurance and teaches about the Christian journey. He brings the believer in contact with other believers through which he might offer teaching, encouragement, and personal testimonies.

The Holy Spirit guides the believer into all truth. Sometimes the truth hurts. The truth can be confrontational by challenging us to examine patterns of ideas, habits and actions inherent in our walk that we might not have considered before. The Holy Spirit dispenses the truth in love so that it should cause us to draw near to God, rather than to run and hide from Him. As we spend time in the habit of bible study and prayer, He reveals the truth with a gradual progression. He weaves it into our daily experiences and teaches us through the trials we experience throughout the day. The more we spend time reading, meditating and memorizing scripture, the more the words of scripture come up as we experience life. I remember discovering that the enemy had devised a plan against me, only after it had failed. The words of the psalmist instantly came to mind:

"You pushed me violently that I might fall, but the Lord helped me."

Psalm 118:13, NKJV

The verse of scripture seemed to spring out of my memory unsummoned. It was the Holy Spirit showing me that God frustrated the plot of the enemy. There was no coincidence. I learned that God was interested in the happenings of my personal life. He was there watching my back. I felt comforted.

As we submit our minds to the study of scripture as a daily habit, the Holy Spirit teaches us on a customized curriculum, designed with the circumstances of daily life. Life doesn't run out of challenges for Him to use as tools for applying the lessons of scripture. Our learning in God is a growth-oriented endeavor, punctuated by moments of struggle and comfort. He is there to illuminate the word in ways that we come to understand it in our heads and experience it in our lives.

"The path of the righteous is like the morning sun, shining ever brighter till the full light of day."

Proverbs 4:18 NIV

There are truths that the Lord in His wisdom chooses to reveal in bits and pieces. These might include revealing the truth about our destiny and mission in life. Had David known ahead of time the struggle he would endure to become a mighty king of Israel, would he have left the simple life of being a shepherd boy? He took steps as God guided him. So it is in the life of every believer. Destiny is written deep in man's spirit, and the Holy Spirit is the searchlight by which it is revealed to his understanding. Nowadays, people suffer at skyrocketing levels from depression and anxiety. A lot of it comes from not knowing what the future holds. The world is changing so quickly. The believer is comforted by having the Holy Spirit illuminate the step-by-step instructions provided in the Word of God. It is a comfort to know that God can be trusted to reveal the next step and that future is secure in Him:

"For I know the plans I have for you," declares the LORD, "plans to prosper you and not to harm you, plans to give you hope and a future."

Jeremiah 29:11 NIV

Few things are more comforting than prayer. A lot of things can be said about the experience of prayer. First, it is engaging and in direct dialogue with the heavenly Father. Second, the results of prayer can be empowerment, encouragement and comfort. Finally, prayer promises to be the cure for anxiety:

"Do not be anxious about anything, but in every situation, by prayer and petition, with thanksgiving, present your requests to God. And the peace of God, which transcends all understanding, will guard your hearts and your minds in Christ Jesus."

Philippians 4:6-7 NIV

The words to say when in need of prayer is not always readily available. When we can't seem to muster the ability to pray for ourselves, it is a comfort to have fellow brothers and sisters nearby to pray on our behalf. What is more remarkable is that the Comforter Himself, the Holy Spirit promises to pray intently on our behalf when we find that we are unable to do so for ourselves:

"Likewise the Spirit helps us in our weakness. For we do not know what to pray for as we ought, but the Spirit himself intercedes for us with groanings too deep for words."

Romans 8:26 ESV

As the believer grows in the spiritual journey with God, fruits become more evident. Righteousness, peace, and joy in the Holy Spirit are the order of each day. The believer is activated in the kingdom. Just like in life, where physical maturity brings about the development of the reproductive system and the desire to reproduce, spiritual maturity brings the believer a desire to make more disciples. Not all believers are called to preach, but all are certainly called to minister in their individual lives.

Ministers of the Gospel are mere pipes and organs. It is the Holy Spirit breathing through them that makes their words effectual.

"While Peter yet spake these words, the Holy Ghost fell on all them which heard the word."

Acts 10:44

When the believer carries the Holy Spirit inside and allows Him to work, the Holy Spirit actively creates opportunities to share the gospel. At any given time, a believer's faith might be challenged, or he or she might be sought out to bear witness for Christ.

"But the Comforter, which is the Holy Ghost, whom the Father will send in my name, he shall teach you all things, and bring all things to your remembrance, whatsoever I have said unto you."

John 14:26

When you are a student, coming into class Monday morning to have the teacher announce a pop-quiz can be nerve-racking, especially if you haven't studied all weekend. There are moments when we are called upon daily to witness, minister or defend our beliefs which can feel much the same. Until we remember we have the Comforter to bring to our memory that which He has been teaching us. This is why it is important that we must nurture a habit of daily bible study so that He will have something to work with. He retrieves what has already been deposited in the data bank, if you will. With His guidance, as we do the work necessary to cultivate the fruit of the Spirit in our lives, witnessing will become easy. It will be a simple matter of sharing what God has done for us.

The ultimate comfort the Holy Spirit provides is the promise of a future resurrection. Many people suffer anxiety because of the fear that death brings. Many of us can recall the first funeral we attended as children. The memories and reactions among people of this first event can range from awe to terror. Perhaps it is the difficulty of grasping the idea that a loved one has gone and will not return. "Well, where did they go?" you might hear a child ask. The experience can be very unsettling at the least. As a result, many people suffer anxiety and depression at the very thought of dying. The Holy Spirit provides the hope of a bodily resurrection to all believers because it is He who resurrected Jesus:

"But if the Spirit of him that raised up Jesus from the dead dwell in you, he that raised up Christ from the dead shall also quicken your mortal bodies by his Spirit that dwelleth in you."

Romans 8:11

The Christian can have peace in facing life's greatest challenge because Jesus defeated death, hades and the grave. The Holy Spirit is constantly there to remind the believer of that victory in Jesus. The fact that the Holy Spirit is even residing inside the believer serves as a guarantee of things to come because it took a miracle for it to happen. The fact that the Holy Spirit inhabits the resurrected spirit of the individual is the greatest evidence for the bodily resurrection to come (2 Corinthians 1:22; Ephesians 1:14) The promise to physical resurrection is the pinnacle blessing in the inheritance of God's children. Being sure of our inheritance offers peace and comfort when faced with the thought of our demise. The Holy Spirit is the one who can bring to mind the reminder that we are God's sons and daughters and heirs to the promise in Christ. He also comforts us when we witness our loved ones who pass on.

Few griefs in life compare to the experience of losing a close relative, especially when it is an untimely death. In such an emotional state of sorrow, even the strongest believer can be tempted with despair. But the Holy Spirit is there to offer comfort and remind the believer of the lessons from scripture:

"Brothers and sisters, we do not want you to be uninformed about those who sleep in death, so that you do not grieve like the rest of mankind, who have no hope. For we believe that Jesus died and rose again, and so we believe that God will bring with Jesus those who have fallen asleep in him. According to the Lord's word, we tell you that we who are still alive, who are left until the coming of the Lord, will certainly not precede those who have fallen asleep. For the Lord himself will come down from heaven, with a loud command, with the voice of the archangel and with the trumpet call of God, and the dead in Christ will rise first. After that, we who are still alive and are left will be caught up together with them in the clouds to meet the Lord in the air. And so we will be with the Lord forever. Therefore encourage one another with these words."

1 Thessalonians 4:13-18 NIV

Throughout their missionary journeys, the disciples were "Looking for that blessed hope, and the glorious appearing of the great God and our Savior Jesus Christ" (Titus 2:13, KJV). It was that hope that most of them used to face a martyr's death unafraid. They reached the known world with the gospel in their time. The Holy Spirit not only empowered them to preach boldly and establish the church worldwide, but He was also responsible for comforting them in their trials with the promise of seeing Jesus and their loved ones again.

They could not have imagined how far the journey of trusting God would take them the night of the last supper. It was a journey that eventually flung each one to the different corners of the known world and into the deep areas of experiencing God's comfort.

Jesus had announced His departure. They had been tempted to feel abandoned. But, Jesus promised:

"I will not leave you orphans; I will come to you."

John 14:18 NKJV

Through the promise of the Comforter, Jesus was able to dwell in them as He had promised. They were able to come to know and experience Him to a greater degree than even when He walked beside them. That night Jesus prayed for them, but He also prayed for you and me. We who have come to believe in Him through the witness of those who were in that room that night, and through the witness of the Holy Spirit. To us, He extends the promise of the Comforter. The Holy Spirit works in a multifaceted way to bring the believer into a continuous encounter and experience with the presence of God. It is impossible to capture and describe exactly what it is like to be moved by Him and to have Him move in and upon us in the pages of any book. It is something that you can only experience on your own account. He has a lifetime of experiences with God available for you. In any endeavor, it is comforting to have a helper that has your back. As you grow in God with the help of the Holy Spirit, you can be confident that not only does He have your rearguard, you are comforted on every side.

When the believer carries the Holy Spirit inside and allows Him to work, the Holy Spirit actively creates opportunities to share the gospel.

***

"But the Comforter, which is the Holy Ghost, whom the Father will send in my name, he shall teach you all things, and bring all things to your remembrance, whatsoever I have said unto you."

John 14:26

"Today, as an adult, I long for more encounters with the Comforter. I long to know Him, not in his power, but as a friend. As I began my ministry, I had an encounter with the Spirit that I later mentioned during a testimony at one of our Sunday services. I was at home praying when the Spirit came upon me suddenly and pressed me into the carpet..."

Chapter 8

A Personal Testimony

He said unto them, Have ye received the Holy Ghost since ye believed? And they said unto him, We have not so much as heard whether there be any Holy Ghost. (Revelation 12:11)

A t the age of five, I was fortunate to witness my mother and father accept salvation and be filled with the Spirit at a tent revival. During that same revival, I saw the Holy Spirit move mightily upon a man. I saw a limb grow spontaneously, a cancer germ die, and other diseases and infirmities cured at a spoken word and the laying of hands. I was amazed; I had never seen anything like that before.

At the age of twelve, in another tent revival, the Holy Spirit arrested me for two weeks. My appetite was taken away, and the Holy Spirit inspired me to fast for two weeks. I know it was a divinely inspired fast because I had no hunger pains. I was so hungry for spiritual nourishment; I anticipated the time I spent with the Lord. Whenever I arrived at the services under that tent, from the opening sound of the music and the singing voices released in the atmosphere, my body shook. Although I did not understand it at the time, it was an intimate encounter with the Holy Spirit. Even then, at twelve years old, the Lord had touched my life in a special way.

Today, as an adult, I long for more encounters with the Comforter. I long to know Him, not in His power, but as a friend. When I began my ministry, I had an encounter with the Spirit that I later mentioned during a testimony at one of our Sunday services. I was at home praying when the Spirit came upon me suddenly and pressed me into the carpet. The power was so physically heavy; it frightened me.

Suddenly, a voice spoke to me and said, "Do not fear; it is me, Jesus. I am sending you to Palm Bay, Florida. I want you to go because there are many in the city I will bring unto you. Go and erect a tabernacle for my people." He told me He was going to give me the house I wanted; He did it. He told me He was going to give me a son; He did it. He also promised to fix my finances—my credit score is over eight hundred. Since that time, miracles, signs and wonders have happened like never before. Although I have not witnessed limbs growing on a person in this ministry, I have witnessed the dilapidated soul saved, the cracked mind delivered, the prostitute transformed, and more. God has completely changed lives through the ministry He has given me, and I know it is by the power of the Holy Spirit.

Personal Relationship

Jesus Christ was completely filled with the Spirit of God. In fact, it was through this power that He was able to keep God's commands. Christ admitted, *"I can of mine own self do nothing: as I hear, I judge: and my judgment is just; because I seek not mine own will, but the will of the Father which hath sent me."* (John 5:30 KJV)

It was through the manifestation of the Holy Spirit and submission to His authority that Jesus was able to teach what He had never learned from books.

It is very important that we submit our will to the Comforter so we do not fall prey to seductive or demonic spirits. It is dangerous to bypass God's order to establish our own. Hence, *"...he gave some, apostles; and some, prophets; and some, evangelists; and some, pastors and teachers; For the perfecting of the saints, for the work of the ministry, for the edifying of the body of Christ." (Ephesians 4:11-12)* God is so mindful of us that He gave these five-fold ministries to the Church to sharpen us, to prevent us from falling away.

One of the pitfalls of the 21st century Church is the desire to eliminate the need for submission and move straight to possessing the power of the Holy Spirit. They would rather be used by God without having an intimate relationship with Him. *"For they being ignorant of God's righteousness, and seeking to establish their own righteousness, have not submitted to the righteousness of God." (Romans 10:3 NKJV)* They prefer to seek God's hand instead of His face. Further, others do not even want mentorship, governance or leadership from anyone in the five-fold ministry. Yet, the Bible instructs, *"Obey them that have the rule over you, and submit yourselves: for they watch for your souls, as they that must give account, that they may do it with joy, and not with grief: for that is unprofitable for you."*

(Hebrews 13:17 KJV)

It is impossible to achieve the will of the Father without submission to the Comforter. Hence, knowledge alone about the Holy Spirit is not sufficient. Believers should recognize and know Him intimately.

Are you submitted to the Holy Spirit? Are you allowing Him to work in your life? Are you letting Him sanctify you? Has He given you power to be an effective witness? Are you manifesting the fruit of the Spirit? Can He speak to you, and you obey? If you have accepted salvation but have not sought the Spirit to be filled, it is similar to standing in a pool without fully submerging yourself. When you submit to the Spirit's power, you lay down your will in exchange for His. You allow Him to cover you in the Spirit then resurrect you with another dimension of power.

The Holy Spirit wants to take personal residence inside you. You can have a joyful life filled with the presence of the Spirit. For this reason, you must listen carefully for the Spirit. He loves to encourage and empower those who are willing to obey His voice as they study Scripture. He has been working from the beginning of time to help Christians, even Jesus, fulfill destiny.

The Commission

Years ago, I had an opportunity to visit Niagara Falls and tour the land. When I arrived, I was amazed by its sound. I stood in awe and watched in admiration. I watched as the water tumbled over the falls, tons of water moving with great strength, velocity and power. I observed the Falls from different levels because it was the only way to truly value its splendor. I studied the water as it was falling. Then, I watched as it hit the base. I even noticed how it flowed over rocks. Despite the amount and size of the rocks, they could not stop the flow of water.

As the Falls hit the base, it resulted in a mist that covered its expanse.

The mist was so heavy it made the public observation area wet; anyone near that area was soaked. Although the actual Falls was a great distance from where I observed, it was so powerful that the mist drenched me. I was surprised by this revelation as well as overwhelmed to see it in operation. Then, the Lord began speaking to my heart about its symbolism and what believers need to embrace.

The water was strong, powerful and limitless. Similarly, Christians must be strong in their faith to overcome adversity. The Bible admonishes, *"Finally, my brethren, be strong in the Lord, and in the power of his might." (Ephesians 6:10 KJV)* With the help of the Comforter, we are able to withstand any test. *"For with God nothing shall be impossible." (Luke 1:37 KJV)* Like the Falls are not deterred by rocks, Christians are also expected to remain steadfast despite dust storms or other barriers. God's Word should propel us to overcome because His promises are *"...yea and in him Amen..." (II Corinthians 11:20).* We are supposed to face barriers and keep flowing over them in power.

The sound of Niagara Falls reminded me of a scripture in the book of Revelation: *"His head and his hairs were white like wool, as white as snow; and his eyes were as a flame of fire; And his feet like unto fine brass, as if they burned in a furnace; and his voice as the sound of many waters." (Revelation 1:14-15 KJV)* If you receive God's word, there is no reason to fear. Like the Falls, His voice alone is enough to instill faith because it is reassuring and full of majestic power. The voice of the Lord divides flames of fire and splinters the cedars of Lebanon. (Psalm 29)

After my visit to Niagara Falls, I later had a vision of me trying to stand under the Falls. In reality, I know I would have been washed away. However, in the vision, I believed I could stand. I heard the Lord say, "You have the power of the Holy Spirit working in you so there are some things you should not be entangled with." As a result, I was encouraged and stood firm under the heavy flowing water.

In this vision, I also saw all nations come to Niagara Falls. Again, the Lord spoke to me and said, "This is what can happen if the truth of the Word is revealed—an insurmountable amount of my presence flowing through your church." This level of God's presence can attract every nation to the house of God. As a result, barriers will be torn, issues broken and healing will take place.

Jesus commissioned, *"...and you shall be witnesses to Me in Jerusalem, and in all Judea and Samaria, and to the end of the earth." (Acts 1:8 NKJV)* This is the assigned work for all believers. Accepting this commission means to become a member of the body of Christ. And as such, all systems are subject to the Head. By the power of the Holy Spirit, we are empowered to encourage one another to strengthen the body. Additionally, like the natural body, we must work together to testify of God's love and help facilitate the extension of God's forgiveness and salvation for unbelievers worldwide.

Looking back on my childhood, I recall the power of God working through the man of God at our church. I remember the phenomenon of witnessing him being used powerfully by God and how it impacted those in attendance. However, he failed to explain that the Holy Spirit was for every believer. Hence, we grew up thinking it was a special power unique to him. We believed he had an anointing that no one else could possess. Thankfully, I have come to understand that our thinking simply was not true. Since Jesus' return to heaven, The

Comforter has come and is available to all His children. Every man, woman, boy, and girl has an opportunity to be filled, baptized and empowered by the Holy Spirit to do mighty exploits in this present world.

TRUTH REVEALED

Bishop Merton Clark's ministry Truth Revealed Int'l Ministries locates the unchurched to teach, train, and develop them to be Disciples of the Lord Jesus Christ. The ministry seeks to change lives by reforming minds to transform communities and advance the Kingdom.

With earnest expectation, we embrace where the Holy Spirit is taking us to change lives, strengthen families, and enrich communities. We are walking in the total unfolding of God's plan for our ministry as we seek to fulfill the cultural mandate.

We use various strategies, approaches, and resources to reach and equip as many people as possible to achieve our goal through a local presence with a global impact.

Community Impact

HELPS Community Initiatives (HCI) is a 501(c)(3) organization that aims to heal every life with purpose and support. HCI is equipped with the knowledge and tools to forge partnerships and build strong social service delivery systems. Services include tutoring programs, career development, jails and prison visitation, nursing home visitation, and a cold night shelter.

Multimedia

Thousands of individuals experience the *Word of Truth Revealed with Bishop Merton Clark* through the daily radio broadcast playing on radio outlets in various cities, including Mobile, Chattanooga,

Richmond, Alexandria, and many more. The broadcast is also available online via your desktop PC or mobile device. You can also listen to the daily broadcast by downloading the Truth Revealed app for free in the App store.

Resource Development

Bishop Merton Clark publishes Revealed magazine online and in printed format monthly. The magazine covers ministry news, community guides, entertainment, sermon aids, and articles with practical advice to strengthen individuals' walk with God and service to others.

Leadership Training

The Sword of the Spirit School of Ministry facilitates educational programs that embody the Word of God and include coursework for personal, spiritual, and professional development. Some courses are valued for Continuing Education Unit as well as viable in transferring for college credit.

Kingdom Keys for Business offers motivating modules to sharpen your ability to think, analyze, and identify the vital determining factors and profitability principles as an entrepreneur. These keys to success are relevant at every stage of your business life and business strategy.

Ministers Enrichment Training prepares those who have declared a calling to advance ministry work to enhance and develop a level of effectiveness, competence, and aspiring ministry persons. The training courses provide the necessary tools for achieving and ensuring ministry practice and protocol in all areas.

Leadership Solutions equip leaders who develop and discipline other leaders to build a savvy team with strong business acumen to create a mission-focused and results-driven culture. Bishop Clark's expertise and experience provide the tools to develop appropriate competencies required for success and measurement of a leader's capabilities.

Abishai Inspired Men (AIM), facilitated by Bishop Merton Clark, honors fathers, build brothers, and mentor sons through monthly meetings. AIM offers an annual conference, Men's Advanced Reloaded, with sessions filled with critical information on medical moments (men's health), mentoring moments, and financial IQ.

Awaken Women's Ministry, founded by Bishop Merton Clark and facilitated by Pastor Sebrena Clark, provides monthly fellowships with encouragement, counseling, and spiritual resources. The fellowships focus on helping women care for their emotional, spiritual, and physical well-being. Awaken Women also offers an annual summit held each year with intensive workshops and resources on faith, family, fitness, and finance.

Bishop Merton Clark is the founder and senior pastor of Truth Revealed International Ministries, a global ministry dedicated to locating the unchurched, teaching, training, and developing them to be Disciples of the Lord Jesus Christ. For almost three decades, Bishop Clark has been fully committed to changing lives by reforming minds to transform communities and advance the Kingdom. His radio program, the *Word of Truth Revealed with Bishop Merton Clark*, is heard daily on several radio outlets and online. Bishop Clark serves as the chaplain for the City of Palm Bay Fire Department. He is married to Sebrena, his wife and ministry partner of more than twenty-eight years. They are the proud parents of two, Omar and Megan, and grandparents to one, Isaiah. For more information, visit mertonclarkpublishing.com.

You are invited to email or write the author with comments about this book. You are also welcome to contact Bishop Clark's office for bookings. Bishop Clark is available for media interviews, book club presentations, book signings, or speaking engagements for your group or organization (conferences, workshops, retreats, seminars, etc.).

Visit Bishop Clark's website at:

mertonclarkpublishing.com

Email:
bishop@truthrevealed.org

Mailing Address:
P.O. Box 60128, Palm Bay, FL 32906

Phone:
(321) 952-5151

Connect with Bishop Clark on social media:

Facebook:
facebook.com/BishopMertonClark

Instagram:
instagram.com/mertonclark/

Twitter:
twitter.com/BshpMerton